CONTRACTS

Series Interior Design: adapted from a design by Roslyn M. Stendahl, Dapper Design
Composition and Imaging by Carlisle Communications

WEST'S COMMITMENT TO THE ENVIRONMENT
In 1906, West Publishing Company began recycling materials left over from the production of books. This began a tradition of efficient and responsible use of resources. Today, 100% of our legal bound volumes are printed on acid-free, recycled paper consisting of 50% new fibers. West recycles nearly 22,650,000 pounds of scrap paper annually—the equivalent of 187,500 trees. Since the 1960's, West has devised ways to capture and recycle waste inks, solvents, oils, and vapors created in the printing process. We also recycle plastics of all kinds, wood, glass, corrugated cardboard, and batteries, and have eliminated the use of polystyrene book packaging. We at West are proud of the longevity and the scope of our commitment to the environment.

West pocket parts and advance sheets are printed on recyclable paper and can be collected and recycled with newspapers. Staples do not have to be removed. Bound volumes can be recycled after removing the cover.

Production, Prepress, Printing and Binding by West Publishing Company.

 TEXT IS PRINTED ON 10% POST CONSUMER RECYCLED PAPER

COPYRIGHT © 1997 by West Professional Training Programs, Inc.
901 Fifteenth Street NW
Washington, D.C. 20005
1-800-6-WESTBAR

ISBN 0-314-20542-X

Brief Contents

Introduction

Contracts

Introductory Material

First Year Key Review: Contracts is provided by West Bar Review to *assist* you, a first-year law student, in the study of the law of Contracts. It is intended and written for use as a *supplement* to your casebook, hornbooks, classroom notes, and other materials your professor requires or suggests that you consult. In all law school courses, your primary sources of information should be the casebook, hornbooks, class notes, and other material cited by your professor. In short, this book should be used only as a *study aid,* not as a substitute for other material. Most students should be able to obtain additional understanding and insight with *First Year Key Review: Contracts.*

In light of the number of Contracts casebooks in use in American law schools, and the sometimes different approach to the subject taken by individual law professors, it was not possible to construct a supplement that will be of assistance in all aspects of Contracts as it is taught in your law school. Nevertheless, the material set forth in *First Year Key Review: Contracts* will relate to a significant part of the material covered in most first-year Contracts courses.

A word about our icons: We have included symbols to signal certain significant portions of this study aid. These include Leading Case, Classroom Notes, Exam Tip, and Major Rule. Leading Case means that you are likely to encounter this case either in your casebook or in classroom discussion. This icon will assist you in putting that case in the context of the subject. There is likely to be a lot of classroom discussion in Contracts on the status of the law, majority and minority holdings, policy considerations, and rationales for rules. The icon Classroom Notes should provide thought-provoking material for those discussions, as well as information that may be used for exams. Major Rule means just what it says; that icon denotes a "black letter" statement of the rule of law. When words are in bold within a Major Rule, those words represent elements of the rule to which you should pay special attention. Exam Tip is also self-explanatory and should be helpful to you when you are under the pressure of studying for your exams. In line with the current trend in first-year examinations the Exam Tips address multiple-choice as well as more traditional essay questions.

In addition to our icons, we have included other features to assist you. When a word or legal term is first used in this study aid, it will appear in blue. This alerts you that a complete definition of that word or legal term can be found in the Glossary. Additionally, you will find West Key Numbers for various topics in Contracts. The Key Numbers will provide a useful starting point for additional in-depth research that you choose to do in particular aspects of this course. The West Key Number System is a helpful research tool that will assist you during your entire legal career (see p. vi for explanation of the West Key Number System). The first year of law school is a great place to master the Key Number System and this study aid will help you do just that.

We have also included Essay Test Questions and Model Answers; these examples should show you how to apply the material learned in class and from both other sources and this study aid on your exams. Should you need to cross-reference a particular case to the relevant portion of this book, consult the Table of Cases. Any important sections of the Uniform Commercial Code are reprinted in the Appendix.

West Bar Review wishes you the best of luck during your first year of law school.

Stanley D. Chess
CEO, West Bar Review

Steven H. Levine
President, West Bar Review

West Key Number System

At the end of most sections you will find references to the Key Number System, the master classification system of U.S. law created and maintained by West Publishing for over 100 years. West divides American case law into more than 400 topics (such as Contracts, Sales, and Damages) and further subdivides each topic into headings, subheadings, and individual key numbers. The key numbers represent the finest level of classification for each point of law headnoted by West editors; users of WESTLAW, West Publishing's on-line computer-assisted legal research service, have access to over 15 million headnotes each with its own key number classification.

The Key Number System performs several important functions in legal research. It permits the user to retrieve cases dealing with particular concepts regardless of the language a judge may have used to express those concepts. Without the Key Number System, cases will be missed where the terms in the user's search request differ from the precise terms used by the court.

The Key Number System also provides a context for terms with multiple meanings and words that appear frequently in case law databases (such as jury, evidence, trial, appeal, etc.). The presence of such ambiguous or common terms in a search request will inundate the user with irrelevant documents unless the user takes advantage of key number references.

References to the Key Number System in this outline may be to headings or subheadings of a topic rather than to individual key numbers, indicating that cases bearing on a particular issue may be classified to a range of key numbers. These headings are denoted by combinations of Roman numerals, letters and numbers. For example, 95II(A) means the topic Contracts (topic number 95), II. Construction and Operation, (A) General Rules of Construction.

Where individual key numbers are given, they appear in two formats: the name of the topic followed by the key number within that topic, and the topic and key numbers separated by the letter **k**, which is the format required for WESTLAW or West CD-ROM research. For example, the following two formats both express the topic Contracts, key number 149:

Contracts ☞ 149

95k149

Use of the topic number in electronic research is generally more precise than use of the topic name.

For instructions on how to use key numbers in a WESTLAW search, consult the WESTLAW Reference Manual. For West CD-ROM Reporters and Digests, consult the PREMISE User Manual. The entire key number classification hierarchy can be viewed on WESTLAW by accessing the KEY service or by viewing **Outline of the Law** on a West CD-ROM Digest.

Contracts

THE RIGHT TO CONTRACT
If a man improvidently bind himself up by a voluntary deed ...
this court will not loose the fetters.
—Lord Nottingham, *Villers v. Beaumont* (1682).

PART ONE—PRELIMINARY MATTERS

I. The Study of Contracts

A contract is defined as a set of promises for the breach of which the law gives a remedy or for the performance of which the law recognizes a duty. It can also be seen as a legal relationship, consisting of the rights and duties of contracting parties. When parties exchange promises—and the promises are legally enforceable—a contract is formed. It is that simple, and that complex.

You already know contracts. You created one when you became a law student. In applying for admission, you offered to attend law school. Such an offer begins the formation of a contract. Your letter of acceptance completed the contract. The mutual contract terms are: You promise to pay tuition and attend classes; the school promises to provide a legal education.

The principles of contract law simply correspond to human relationships. These concepts are not arcane abstractions. After all, the purpose of contract law is to facilitate the formation of mutually beneficial agreements. To accomplish this goal, the law of contracts has developed a distinctive language. It must be learned as a law student and applied when you practice as an attorney.

Contract law is an essential part of any first-year law school curriculum. The study of contracts is typically based upon an analysis of ground breaking cases from England and the United States. These real-life disputes have generated the body of law which defines and regulates the world of contracts. Law professors also engage students in the solution of hypothetical problems in order to develop analytical skills. The ability to understand patterns of behavior is as crucial as a grasp of contract language. Ultimately both skills are needed to understand and express the essence of contracts.

II. Constitutional Considerations

The right to make contracts is fundamentally rooted in the U.S. Constitution (Article I, § 10). Many state constitutions also provide parallel support for contract rights. The ability to freely contract is nothing less than the ability to organize one's own personal and business affairs. This is a strongly protected prerogative. Governments are not completely prohibited from regulating private agreements. However, they can do so only if there is a compelling public need, such as the necessity of preventing fraud. Even then, laws regulating contracts are only constitutional to the extent necessary to protect that public need. Short of those severe circumstances, private parties are free to contract as they wish.

West's Key No. Digests, Constitutional Law ⬫ 114, 145-185. (92k114, 92VII(C))

III. The Common Law

The *common law* of contracts has been generated by accumulated court decisions. This body of law emerged when courts in the past were asked to make judgments about contract disputes. These judgments were not created from scratch, but were based on *precedent*—the decisions of previous courts in similar cases. These in turn recognized the business customs which were the product of centuries of commerce.

The common law has been organized into certain widespread legal principles, such as *offer* and *acceptance* mentioned above. In recent years, the common law of contracts has lost some of its importance as contracts for the sale of goods are now covered by a statute—the Uniform Commercial Code. Nevertheless, common law principles still cover all other contracts including the sale of real estate, services, and intangible property. In addition, common law principles have had a great influence on the specific rules regulating the sale of goods found in the Uniform Commercial Code.

IV. The Restatement

The Restatement (Second) of Contracts is a treatise on contracts published by the American Law Institute (referred to here simply as *R2d*). The Restatement sets out the common law rules of contract law followed in a majority of U.S. jurisdictions. While not itself a statute, it is frequently relied on by courts and cited by them as authoritative. Its influence is pervasive in part because it helps bring order to the somewhat inconsistent common law.

The Restatement came into being in response to the difficulty courts and lawyers sometimes faced in ascertaining the status of the common law rules. The Restatement sets out a set of uniform principles of liability, performance, and remedies for breach of contract. This helps to harmonize legal principles and business practices.

V. The Uniform Commercial Code

The sale of tangible goods is addressed by a special statute called the *Uniform Commercial Code* (referred to simply as the *UCC*). The UCC largely follows the common law, but extends its reach. It prevails over the common law when they conflict. This outline supplies principles which apply to both UCC and common law situations.

The UCC was drafted by the National Conference of Commissioners on Uniform State Laws and the American Law Institute, and has been adopted by all states. Article 2 of the UCC regulates the sale of goods, i.e., tangible, movable, personal property. Leases of goods are not covered. For a mixed sale of both goods and services, the UCC applies only if goods predominate.

When one or both contracting parties is a merchant—a business person—the UCC provides additional rules to facilitate commerce. For example, an agreement between merchants can be determined not only from the contract language, but also from the previous course of dealing, usage of trade, or course of performance. This enhances the flow of commerce by allowing legal reliance on past experience between the parties, or in the field of business. For definitions, see p. 149, **Appendix B: Glossary**.

VI. The Burden of Proof

Contract disputes are a matter of civil law, as opposed to criminal law. In most cases, the presumption is that agreements between consenting adults are valid. The level of proof needed to prove a point or a fact is usually a *preponderance of the evidence,* as opposed to *beyond a reasonable doubt*. This preponderance standard means that it is more likely than not that the point was proven. The weight of the evidence must slightly tip the scales of justice in its direction.

An even heavier burden is shouldered by anyone attempting to show that a contract is illegal, when it appears innocent according to its terms (*prima facie*). In that case, the presumption that the contract is legal can only be defeated by *clear and convincing* evidence. This test demands stronger proof than a preponderance but less than proof beyond a reasonable doubt as in criminal cases. Clear and convincing evidence makes an assertion highly probable, and produces a firm conviction about the truth of the assertion.

Interpretation of an unambiguous contract is always done by the court, i.e., a judge. This is also true when any ambiguity is explained away by uncontradicted external (*extrinsic*) evidence. In these cases, a jury has no job to do. On the other hand, when a contract is ambiguous, it is the responsibility of the jury to interpret the terms and resolve the ambiguities.

West's Key No. Digests, Contracts ☞ 28(1), 348. (95k28(1), 95k348)

VII. Summary of Contract Law

This summary presents a condensed overview of the birth, life span, and completion of a contract. Each section is expanded in the detailed outline, in the same order. They are presented roughly chronologically, like the order in which the different aspects of actual contracts are addressed. *Specialized legal terms are italicized.*

A. CONTRACT FORMATION

■ **1. Offer**

Contract logic is the logic of human relationships. It mirrors the bargains we strike in ordinary daily life. The opening move to make (*form*) a contract is an *offer.* It has to be more than mere musing or a negotiating gambit. If a student says to a group of people at a party: "I'd love to sell my old sports car," that is not specific enough to be a contract offer—it is just an invitation to the party-goers to negotiate. The one making an offer is the *offeror.* A valid offer must show an immediate readiness (*manifest a present willingness*) to form a contract, as opposed to an intention to make a commitment in the future; the offer must have definite enough terms such as the names of the contracting parties; and the offer must be known to the *offeree(s)* to whom it is directed.

West's Key No. Digests, Contracts ⬥ 16. (95k16)

■ **2. Acceptance**

Once an offer is made, it can be accepted until it is withdrawn (*terminated*). *Acceptance* means that the party to whom the offer was directed consents to its terms and agrees to form the proposed contract. An offer can be terminated in a number of ways. For example, an offer automatically will be terminated if a time for expiration is included in the offer and that time occurs before an acceptance. If an offer is accepted before termination, the next issue is whether there is good *consideration.*

West's Key No. Digests, Contracts ⬥ 16, 22. (95k16)

■ **3. Consideration**

Consideration means that there has to be some exchange of benefits between the parties. If you say to a friend: "I'll sell you my old sports car," and the friend says: "I accept," that is not yet a contract because there is no consideration included for you, the seller. There has to be joint benefit (*mutuality*). If you say to a classmate: "I will sell you my sports car for $400," and he says "It's a deal," there is mutual consideration and a contract has been formed.

West's Key No. Digests, Contracts ☞ 47-91. (95I(D))

B. CONTRACT INTERPRETATION

■ 1. Express—Implied—Quasi

After forming a contract, many issues can arise over its interpretation. There are explicit (*express*) contracts manifested by oral or written words; *implied* contracts, formed by the behavior of the contracting parties; and *quasi* contracts, created by law when necessary to avoid unjust enrichment. Here are examples of each.

> **EXAMPLES:** (1) A student says to a classmate: "I'll sell you my old sports car for $400," and the classmate says: "I accept." They draw up and sign an agreement. That is an *express* contract.
> (2) A patron says to a waiter: "I want the spaghetti marinara." This is the acceptance of an *implied* contract offer. The patron's promise to pay the menu price is *implied* by his order.
> (3) A bleeding person rushes to a hospital and is treated. The patient's conduct creates a *quasi* contract. The patient must pay for the treatment, even though there is no formal contract.

West's Key No. Digests, Contracts ☞ 3, 27; Implied and Constructive Contracts ☞ 2. (95k3, 95k27, 205Hk2)

■ 2. Divisible—Entire

Some contracts are divisible into independent acts, each of which confers a separate benefit, and for which a separate payment is deserved. These are *divisible* contracts. In that case, the completion (*performance*) of each separate act triggers the payment of consideration, as seen below.

> **EXAMPLE:** A student says to a classmate: "I'll make you dinner each Friday this winter, for $20 per meal," and the classmate says: "I accept." Payment is due after each meal, not in the spring.

Other contracts are entire or nondivisible. In this case, only substantial completion (*substantial performance*) of the entire contract triggers the payment of consideration.

> **EXAMPLE:** A student says to a classmate: "I'll cater your graduation dinner on Friday for $200," and the classmate says: "I accept." Payment is due only after the entire meal, not after just one or two courses.

West's Key No. Digests, Contracts ☞ 171. (95k171)

■ 3. Bilateral—Unilateral

A *bilateral* contract is formed when two parties exchange mutually dependent promises, such as: "I will sell you my old sports car on Friday if you will pay me $400," and in return: "I will pay you the $400 on Friday if you will sell the sports car to me." When the promises are exchanged, the contract is formed—even though the promises themselves are ultimately fulfilled later.

A *unilateral* contract is formed when one party offers to perform, and invites a performance—not a promise. The second party can *only* accept by performing.

> **EXAMPLE:** A student says to a friend: "I'll pay you $20 if you make me dinner this Friday." The student-offeror is not asking for a promise, but for a meal. The friend can ignore the offer, but can accept it only by actually making the dinner. Even if the friend says: "I promise to make the meal on Friday," there is still no contract until the food is served.

This bilateral-unilateral distinction is not true for transactions covered by the UCC. The UCC, designed to advance the cause of commerce, wants to facilitate contract formation. Accordingly, in most instances, it allows acceptance by either performance or a return promise. This is feasible because merchants are more concerned about the efficient flow of business, rather than the formality of contract principles.

> **EXAMPLE:** A manufacturer sends an offer to purchase 1,000 ball-bearings from a distributor. The distributor can accept either by shipping the bearings, or by promising to ship them within a reasonable time. Either action forms a binding contract.

West's Key No. Digests, Contracts ☞ 15. (95k15)

■ 4. The Parol Evidence Rule

The purpose of this rule of law is to prevent disputes over the meaning of written contracts. Under the *parol evidence rule*, if the parties have reduced their agreement to writing, which they intend to be final and complete, they cannot contradict or change it with evidence of prior oral or written or contemporaneous oral agreements.

> **EXAMPLE:** A student says to a friend: "I'll sell you my old sports car for $400," and the friend says: "I accept." They draw up and sign a complete, written contract. Later, the friend claims that the student had also agreed by phone to accept an old Ford as a trade-in. The trade-in is not part of the contract.

West's Key No. Digests, Evidence ☞ 384-469. (157XI)

C. DEFENSES TO CONTRACT FORMATION

It sometimes happens that even after there has been an offer, an acceptance, and there is consideration, a party may not want a contract to be enforced. In those cases, the party may try to nullify a supposed contract by raising certain defenses. First, there are *formation defenses*. For example, a contract cannot be formed by a person previously adjudicated by a court to be mentally unable to make or understand a contract. Any supposed contract made by him is void from the beginning. There are also *public policy defenses,* such as illegality.

> **EXAMPLE:** A homeowner says to a thug: "I'll pay you $500 to torch my house for the insurance." The thug agrees. There is no contract because the law won't enforce an illegal act.

Other defenses to contract formation include *enforcement defenses,* based on the *Statute of Frauds*.

This statute requires a written contract in circumstances in which contracts are very valuable (such as the sale of land) or if contracts are easily but falsely assumed to exist (such as promises made in consideration of marriage). The purpose of this special statute is to avoid perjury and prevent dubious claims that people might otherwise be tempted to make. If any of these defenses are successful, the contract to which they apply becomes unenforceable, and the parties do not have to fulfill their promises.

D. CONTRACT CONDITIONS

Conditions modify the promises contained in a contract. Conditions must be either *excused* or *satisfied*. If a student contracts to "sell his sports car for $400, as soon as I buy a new car," the new car purchase is a condition to the sale of the sports car. If the new car is bought, the condition has been satisfied, and the duty to sell the sports car has come due and must be performed. Conditions can also be excused, for example, by *waiver*. A waiver is the voluntary relinquishment of a known right. Even if a contract states a certain deadline, the parties can mutually agree to extend it, thus waiving the original condition.

Other conditions are inserted by law. For example, when a prospective home owner signs a contract to purchase a home, the purchase is often dependent on whether financing is obtained by the purchaser. The law implies the condition of a good faith effort by the purchaser to obtain the financing. If the purchaser makes no effort, the *implied condition* is breached, and the purchaser may be liable to the seller for any resulting loss, or *damages*.

West's Key No. Digests, Contracts ☜ 218-227. (95II(E))

E. DISCHARGE OR PERFORMANCE OF CONTRACTS

Once contract formation comes this far, there has been an offer, an acceptance in return, consideration given, and conditions have been satisfied or excused, now the duties the contract contains must be either discharged or performed. There are several justifications provided by law which discharge parties' contract duties. One example is *impossibility*. This occurs when no reasonable person could objectively be expected to any longer perform the contract. This can only be so because of an unforeseeable, intruding (*supervening*) event which occurred after the contract was formed.

> **EXAMPLE:** A student said to a friend: "I'll sell you my old sports car on Friday for $400," and the friend said: "I accept." They draw up and sign a complete, written contract. Unfortunately, the car then was stolen and was still missing on Friday. The duty to perform according to the contract was discharged.

Most contracts require merely substantial—not perfect—performance, which meets the essential, if not the trifling, demands of a contract. When perfect performance is required, it must be unequivocally spelled out as an *express* condition. If performance is insufficient or defective, a *breach of contract* occurs. The law then provides various remedies to cure the injured party.

West's Key No. Digests, Contracts ☜ 275-323. (95V)

F. REMEDIES FOR BREACH OF CONTRACT

There are two kinds of remedies for breach of contract: *Legal* and *equitable*. The legal remedy is money damages. Through an award of money, the law tries to restore any wronged parties to the position they would have been in, had the contract not been breached. The remedy attempts to give the benefit of the bargain to the innocent party who was not in breach of the contract. The most common type of money damages is called *expectation damages*—what the contracting party *expected* to receive as a benefit from the contract. These damages must be reasonably calculated and not speculative, i.e., dependent upon future developments which are purely contingent or conjectural.

EXAMPLE: A student signed a contract to sell his old sports car for $400. Later, the buyer refused to complete the sale. The student could sell the car elsewhere for only $300. The student's damages are the difference between the expected $400 from the contract, and the $300 actually received.

In addition, because the student made $100 less, he missed the chance to invest in Netscape stock and earn a $5,000 profit. However, this is too speculative to count as damages, and the added $5,000 will not be awarded to the student.

In contrast, equitable remedies are ordered by a court only when there is no adequate legal remedy. If you contract to buy a unique property, for example, no amount of money can substitute. Two types of equitable remedies are *injunctions* and *specific performance*. They are used by courts to make the parties to a contract fulfill their duties, when money cannot repair the harm caused by a breach of the contract.

EXAMPLE: An attorney signs a contract to purchase an historic house previously owned by the esteemed Professor Kingsfield. Later, the seller decides he could make a lot more selling the house elsewhere. The buyer can ask a court for an injunction to prevent the seller from transferring the house to anyone else and for specific performance, ordering the seller to transfer the house to the buyer.

West's Key No. Digests, Contracts ⌫ 324-355. (95VI)

G. THE RIGHTS AND DUTIES OF NONPARTIES

Agreements made between contracting parties usually do not create rights and duties in other third parties. However, they can create such rights in certain exceptional contracts. One type of nonparty who can receive a benefit from a contract is a *third-party beneficiary*. When a contract between two parties is intended for the benefit of a third person, the third person acquires contract rights. For example, if a son contracts with a landscaping service to have his mother's lawn mowed every week, Mom is the intended third-party beneficiary. She stands in the shoes of her son, the *offeror*, and has an enforceable right to the benefits of the contract.

Only *intentional* beneficiaries have such enforceable rights. For example, if there is a service station where the landscaper who cuts Mom's lawn buys gasoline, the service station would also benefit from the contract. However, the service station has no enforceable rights because it is only an unintended (*incidental*) beneficiary, who is neither named in the contract, nor who the contracting parties intend to benefit.

Assignments are another means of creating third-party rights. Parties to a contract often can assign a right they have to another. An assignment transfers the benefit of a contract from the original contracting party to a nonparty. Assignments sometimes can be prohibited in a contract or by statute. They can also be prohibited if they increase the burden or risks of the *obligor*—the one from whom the benefit is due.

> **EXAMPLES:** (1) A student says to a friend: "I'll sell you my old sports car for $400," and the friend says: "I accept." They draw up and sign a complete, written contract. The student (the *assignor*) then assigns the $400 to her sister (the *assignee*) to pay a debt already owed to the sister. The buyer (the *obligor*) would then pay the $400 directly to the sister.
>
> (2) However, if the student had originally agreed to take a personal check from the buyer (the *obligor*), but the sister insisted upon a cashier's check which would cost more, this would be an added burden upon the obligor, and would be invalid.

Delegations are a means of creating third-party duties. Parties to a contract can sometimes delegate a duty. A delegation transfers the duty to perform a contract from the original contracting party to another, who assumes responsibility. Delegations can be prohibited in the contract or by statute. They can also be prohibited if they decrease the value to the *obligee*—the one to whom the duty is owed.

> **EXAMPLES:** (1) A student says to a classmate: "I'll cater your graduation dinner on Friday for $200," and the friend says: "I accept," forming a contract. The student (the *delegant*) then delegates, for consideration, the catering job to a friend (the *delegate*), who must perform the catering duty. The classmate can enforce the contract against either the student-delegant or the delegate-friend.
>
> (2) However, if the friend was a less skilled chef than the original student, this would be an extra loss to the obligee (the graduate) and the delegation would be invalid.

West's Key No. Digests, Contracts ☞ 185-188.5. (95k185 to 95k188.5)

PART TWO—CONTRACT FORMATION

OVERVIEW:
A contract is a set of voluntary, exchanged promises that the law will enforce. If a promise made in a contract is broken, there is a breach, for which the law provides remedies. The law intervenes because it recognizes the validity of the promises or duties imposed by the contract. There are three basic requirements for a valid contract: offer, acceptance, and consideration.

I. The Offer

A. OPENING GAMBIT

An offer is the opening move made by an *offeror* to an *offeree* in order to form a contract. It shows that the offeror is ready to make a deal. This is also known as *manifesting a present willingness*. The offer must justifiably convince the offeree that consent to the bargain will form a contract. In other words, it leads the offeree to understand that the offeror wants to make an agreement on the terms offered.

B. EFFECT

A valid offer empowers and permits an offeree to accept it. The offeror is master of the offer, and can revoke it before acceptance, except in the case of *option contracts*, when an offeree has separately paid to make the offer irrevocable, or in the case of a *merchant's firm offer* under the UCC.

C. OBJECTIVE INTENT

In determining whether an offer has been made, courts focus on the outward, objective expression (*manifestation of assent*) of the offeror. Subjective intent is not controlling. An offeror's real, but unexpressed, state of mind is usually immaterial.

> **CASEBOOK EXAMPLE:** *Embry v. Hargardine*, 105 S.W. 777 (Mo. App. 1907)
> An employee was negotiating a renewal of his contract. The employer assured him that his contract would be renewed, but confidentially intended to terminate him. The employee sued after being laid off, and the court ruled that the objective expression of intent governed, and the employment contract was renewed.

West's Key No. Digests, Contracts ☞ 14. (95k14)

D. REASONABLE PERSON STANDARD

In case of a dispute, an offer is interpreted to mean what a reasonable person, in the position of the offeree, would conclude it to mean. Courts consider what the offeree knows or should have known about the intention of the offeror. The actual mental agreement of the parties is not required. Thus, there need be no actual meeting of minds.

> **EXAMPLE:** Jethro, after drinking too much, offers to sell Clem his new tractor in exchange for Clem's hunting cap. Clem, a sober farmhand, knows that Jethro is kidding. Jethro's statement is not a true offer to form a contract.

E. THREE REQUISITES

An offer must constitute a commitment to make a deal; it must contain definite terms such as the names of the contracting parties; and it must be communicated to an identifiable offeree.

■ 1. Offeror's Commitment

The offer must show a present willingness to do, or refrain from doing, some act which the offeror has a legal right to do, or has a good faith belief in having the right to do. The commitment must be a positive expression of intention to act or refrain from acting. This commitment can be manifested by language or circumstances.

West's Key No. Digests, Contracts ☞ 16. (95k16)

a. When Made or Written

Most offers can be spoken or in writing, although, as will be discussed below, some offers must be in writing. A problem sometimes arises when there has been a verbal agreement later reduced to a writing, even though the writing was not required by law. If the parties intended to form a contract at the time of the verbal agreement—the writing simply was to memorialize the event—the spoken offer and acceptance are valid and a verbal contract was formed. If, however, the parties intended that the agreement was not valid until the writing, no verbal contract was formed.

In determining the intent of the parties, courts will consider such factors as whether:

- indispensable terms were already reached;
- it was the type of contract often put in writing;
- it was not very detailed or unusual; or
- either party prepared for performance (R2d § 28, Comment c).

b. Advertisements

Advertisements are usually not offers, but invitations for offers, because they are too indefinite. This normally includes quoting a price for a product without further elaboration. However, an advertisement that is definite, explicit, identifies the offeree, and leaves nothing open for negotiation, may be considered an offer.

> **EXAMPLE:** A store advertised: "Nationally famous suits. Normally at $250, today only $150." A customer who showed up and offered $150 could not enforce a contract for purchase of a suit, in part because no quantity was mentioned.

CASEBOOK EXAMPLE: *Lefkowitz v. Great Minn. Surplus Stores*, 86 N.W. 689 (Minn. 1957)
A store advertised: "3 Black Lapin Stoles, Beautiful, Worth Up to $139, $1 First-Come First-Served." The first customer to the store offered the $1, but the store refused to provide the stole. A court ruled that an enforceable contract existed for purchase of the stole.

c. Auctions

There are two types of auctions, those *with reserve* and those without. Auctions with reserve may withdraw the auctioned goods at any time prior to completion of the sale. However, if an auctioneer drops the gavel, the last bid has been accepted and a contract is formed (UCC § 2-328).

In an auction explicitly billed as being *without reserve,* after calling for bids the auctioneer cannot then withdraw the goods, unless no bids are received within a reasonable time. In other words, the auction is an irrevocable offer to sell the goods to the highest bidder (UCC § 2-328(3)).

West's Key No. Digests, Auctions and Auctioneers ⟿ 8. (47k8)

d. Bid Solicitations

A party may desire to form a contract in the future and thus solicit bids from others. This constitutes an invitation for preliminary negotiations and is not an offer.

An invitation from a general contractor to a series of subcontractors to bid to supply labor or material for a construction project so that the general contractor could put together her bid for the job is not an offer.

The general contractor only accepts those bids if she got the project.

West's Key No. Digests, Contracts ⟿ 17. (95k17)

e. Frolic and Banter

A party may literally appear to make an offer, but the conduct or circumstances surrounding the proposal indicate to a reasonable person that none was intended.

CASEBOOK EXAMPLE: *Graves v. Northern N.Y. Pub. Co., Inc.*, 22 N.Y.S.2d 537 (Sup. Ct. 1940)
A newspaper—in its joke column—offered $1,000 to anyone who would provide the published telephone number of Western Union. An enterprising reader attempted to collect. The court ruled that the paper never actually intended to offer the $1,000, the plaintiff was put to no disadvantage, and thus there was no valid contract.

f. Mere Opinions

An offer must contain a commitment rather than merely express an opinion. The test is whether a reasonable person in the supposed offeree's position would conclude that the offeror was actually promising certain actions.

> **EXAMPLE:** A student says to a classmate: "I believe my old sports car is worth $400." The classmate says: "I'll take it." There is no contract because the student expressed an opinion, not an offer with the requisite immediate commitment to make a deal.

g. Mere Intentions

A person announcing an intention to form a contract in the future is normally not considered to have made an offer.

> **EXAMPLE:** If a student informs his roommate that he intends to sell his sports car for $400 someday soon, this is not yet an offer, because there is no *present* intention to contract.

h. Mere Predictions

A person expressing a hope for the future is not always making an offer. If a physician says to a patient: "After the operation, you should feel 20 years younger," it is probably not a promise to secure a specific result. However, if the prediction is specific and more pivotal to the parties, it may constitute a contract.

> **CASEBOOK EXAMPLE:** *Hawkins v. McGee,* **84 N.H. 114 (1929)**
> A surgeon told his young patient that after an operation on his scarred hand, it would be "100 percent perfect." It turned out to be hairy, because of the type of skin graft used. The patient sued, and the court ruled that the surgeon's statement was a promise to perform, constituting a valid contract.

■ 2. Definite Terms

The offer must contain definite terms.

Basic terms of a contract offer usually must be definite enough, so that if the offer is accepted and the contract is formed, a court could provide a remedy in case of breach.

If parties attempt to form a contract, but their agreement is too vague, their efforts are futile.

West's Key No. Digests, Contracts ⟜ 9. (95k9)

a. Indispensable Terms

Some aspects of a contract are so basic that if they are omitted from an agreement, it often cannot be enforced as a contract. These include certain indispensable items:

- the parties;
- the things or service due;
- the price; and
- the time for performance.

b. Supplied by the Common Law

Other aspects of a contract are secondary enough that if the parties fail to address them, a court may supply the terms. For common law contracts, there are only limited circumstances when this is done. These *gap-fillers* usually fall into three main categories.

1) Peripheral Terms

If a term is not central, e.g., the time of performance for a service like painting a house, a court may supply a reasonable time.

2) Inadvertently Forgotten

If the parties would have agreed to the term had they considered it, a court may supply it.

> **EXAMPLE:** Ray regularly washed Bert's car and the fee was the same each month. Ray then washed the car again in the same month, though no fee was discussed. A court would assume that the customary fee was inadvertently forgotten but should be paid.

3) Important Public Policy

When an important public policy is at stake, a court may supply a term. Preventing someone from gaining a windfall profit at the expense of another would be one such policy. Thus, when one party has already performed a contract, and it would be otherwise seriously unfair, a court will insert an omitted term. This is called the prevention of *unjust enrichment*.

> **EXAMPLE:** Ray contracts to paint Bert's house, and does, but no fee was stated in the contract. A court would insert a fair fee for Ray, rather than allow Bert a free paint job.

c. Supplied by the UCC

Under the UCC, an offer can be considered valid even though some basic common law indispensable terms are omitted. Thus, agreements for the sale of goods, which are covered by the UCC, can leave many terms to be specified later by the parties in good faith. They must be *commercially reasonable*. The parties must intend to make a contract and there must be a reasonably certain basis for the supplied terms. They must be rationally calculated, and not fanciful or speculative (UCC § 2-204(3)).

> **EXAMPLE:** Vincent owns a paint store. Whistler orders 50 cans of paint, but no price is stated. Based on the UCC, a commercially reasonable price at the time of delivery can be inserted.

1) Quantity Omitted
In the sale of goods, the quantity must be supplied by the contract itself, except for output and requirement contracts. An *output contract* is an agreement to purchase a party's entire output of specified goods. A *requirement contract* is an agreement to supply or take all of a party's requirements for specified goods (UCC § 2-306(1)).

2) Price Omitted
An unspecified price will be estimated as a reasonable price at the time of delivery in certain circumstances:

- if price is not mentioned in an intended contract;
- the price is to be set later, but is not;
- the price is to be set according to some external factor but is not;
- the buyer or seller is to set the price but does not; or
- if the intended party does not set the price in good faith, the other party can cancel the contract or set the price itself.

3) Other Omitted Terms
The applicable usage of trade, course of dealing, or course of performance may be relied on to supply omitted terms. When needed, UCC provisions supply a method to determine:

1. place and time for delivery and payment;
2. passage of title;
3. manner of identification;
4. proposed delivery, i.e., *tender*, by seller; and
5. risk of loss.

See p. 38, **3. Acceptance by Nonconforming Shipment.**

d. Supplied by Conduct
The parties' subsequent conduct can cure a lack of definite terms. Conduct that clarifies an unstated or indefinite material term renders it definite.

EXAMPLE: A grocer makes an agreement with a fruit wholesaler to deliver "Ten bushels of apples per week for 26 weeks, at $10 per bushel." The contract fails to specify the type of apple. However, if the distributor delivers MacIntosh apples, and the grocer accepts them, the contract has been made definite and is then enforceable.

e. Range of Terms

An offer allowing a party to specify a range of choices may be definite enough to form a contract. For example, if an offer provides, "Buyer may purchase any horse on my ranch for $2,000," a valid contract is formed, and is performed when the Buyer chooses a horse.

f. Real Estate Contracts

A real estate contract offer must contain a description of the property sufficient to identify the parcel and the price to be paid.

A price to be agreed upon in the future is insufficient.

g. Employment Contracts

An employment contract offer must describe its duration, either by length (such as a year) or by project (such as to build a house). If no term is specified, the offer will be presumed to be at will, terminable whenever the employer decides.

■ 3. Communication to Offeree

An offer must be communicated to the offeree, who must have actual knowledge of it. An offer is limited (*personal*) to an identified offeree, and cannot be accepted by, or assigned to, another.

EXAMPLE: Ashley sends a fax to cousin Beth: "Beth, I will sell you my sapphire ring for $150." Beth's roommate Carol sees the fax, and responds: "Beth is not here, but I accept your offer and will buy the ring." There is no contract, because the offer was limited to Beth.

West's Key No. Digests, Contracts ⚷ 18. (95k18)

a. Bilateral Offers

A bilateral contract is formed when two or more parties exchange mutually dependent promises. A contract cannot be formed unless both parties are aware of an offer, because a bargained-for exchange would otherwise be absent.

> **EXAMPLE:** A student says to a friend: "I will sell you my old sports car on Friday if you will pay me $400." In response, the friend says: "I will pay you the $400 on Friday for the sports car." The dual promises and benefits form a bilateral contract.

b. Unilateral Offers

A unilateral contract is formed when one party offers to perform, and invites a performance—not a promise. The offeree can only accept by performing. However, an offeree must be aware of the offer and act because of it, so communication to the offeree is still essential.

> **EXAMPLE:** A student says to a friend: "I'll pay you $20 if you make me dinner this Friday." The friend makes the meal on Friday, accepting the offer by his cooking and thus completing the contract.

c. Not Crossing Offers

Even identical offers that cross in the mail do not form a contract, though the parties appear to agree. Because the parties were unaware of the other's offer, they couldn't have consented to it. The mutual, simultaneous agreement which is basic to contracts is missing.

> **NOTE—*Divergent Minority Rule:*** A few jurisdictions do authorize contract formation after crossing offers, reasoning that the parties would have agreed to each other's offers given the chance.

d. Public Offers and Rewards

Although a public offer does not identify a specific offeree, it is valid for anyone who performs the act requested while knowing of the offer.

> **EXAMPLES:** (1) A student posts an announcement: "I will pay $100 for the person who returns my lost contract class notes." The student has a valid contract with anyone who returns the notes knowing of the reward.
>   (2) However, in most states if someone returns the notes while unaware of the offer, the student need not pay. The reward is an offer to form a unilateral contract which can only be accepted knowingly.

Also, if an enterprising classmate made copies of the notes, and tried to return them for multiple rewards, the student need not pay. It is unreasonable to assume that the student intended to allow multiple acceptances. However, in some circumstances, it is reasonable to expect multiple acceptances.

CASEBOOK EXAMPLE: *Carlill v. Carbolic Smoke Ball Co.*, 1 Q.B. 256 (1893)
A company advertised a reward to anyone who contracted influenza after using its medicine, the Carbolic Smoke Ball. Thousands of buyers subsequently got the flu and successfully claimed the reward.

NOTE—*Divergent Minority Rule:* A few jurisdictions do authorize contract formation even when a party *unknowingly* responds to a public offer. These courts reason that since the desired benefit was bestowed upon the offeror, the actor should not be penalized for acting altruistically, rather than in response to the offer.

EXAMPLE: A student posts an announcement: "I will pay $100 for the person who returns my lost contract class notes." A fellow student finds the notes and returns them out of empathy, knowing nothing of the reward. In a minority of jurisdictions, a valid contract has been formed and the student-offeror owes the finder $100.

F. TERMINATION OF AN OFFER

An offer is only valid until it has been withdrawn (*terminated*). An offer otherwise remains open. **Termination** occurs because of the lapse of a specified time or other contract terms, occurrence of subsequent events, or the actions of the parties. The termination cancels the offer, although a new one can always be made.

■ 1. Lapse of Time
An offer naturally terminates at the end of the time stated in the offer. Any effort to accept afterward will be considered a counteroffer.

West's Key No. Digests, Contracts ☞ 20. (95k20)

a. Clock Starts When Received
Unless stated otherwise, the clock starts running when the offeree receives the offer—or should have received it.

EXAMPLES: (1) A contract offer dated March 1 states: "This offer will terminate in 5 days," and the offeree receives it in the mail on March 5. The offeree has until March 10 to accept.
  (2) A contract offer dated March 1 states: "This offer will terminate in 5 days." The offeree receives it in the mail on March 5, but it sits unopened on his desk until March 9. The offeree must still accept by March 10.

b. Reasonable Time Implied
If the duration of the offer is not stated, it will be deemed open for a reasonable time, considering the circumstances (UCC § 2-204).

c. Person-to-Person Negotiations

When parties are negotiating face to face or by telephone, an offer may be made. The parties are free to stipulate on how long an offer remains open for acceptance. However, if no duration is specified, any offer terminates when the meeting or call ends, and cannot be accepted later. Of course, a new offer and acceptance can occur at a later time.

■ 2. Subsequent Events

An offer is automatically terminated by operation of law if either party dies or is incapacitated, the subject matter of the offer is destroyed, or a later change in a statute (*a supervening illegality*) makes the contract illegal.

West's Key No. Digests, Contracts ↫ 20. (95k20)

a. Death or Incapacity

If either party to a contract dies or no longer has the mental capacity to legally contract, the offer is terminated, even if there is a good faith acceptance before the offeree learns of the offeror's death or incapacity. Mental capacity means the ability to understand the nature and effects of one's acts.

One exception: An option contract offer is irrevocable after consideration has been paid (see p. 30, *c. Supervening Illegality*, p. 35, **5. Time of Acceptance and the Mailbox Rule**, and p. 36, **6. Acceptance by Conduct**).

b. Destruction of Subject Matter

The destruction of a person or thing essential for performance of the proposed contract terminates the offer. The subject matter is the contract's central reason for being.

> **EXAMPLE:** A student says to a friend: "I'll sell you my old sports car on Friday for $400." Before the friend accepts, the car is stolen and totaled. The offer is terminated.

c. Supervening Illegality

If a contract becomes illegal after an offer is made but before acceptance, the offer is terminated.

> **EXAMPLE:** A bank offers to lend a student $1,000 at 12 percent interest. The next day Congress passes a consumer lending statute setting a usury ceiling of 11 percent. The offer is terminated.

■ **3. Actions of the Parties**

a. Direct Revocation

An offer is revoked by the offeror when the revocation is communicated to the offeree or the offeree's agent before acceptance (R2d § 42). An offer is also terminated when the offeree indirectly receives news of revocation from any reliable source.

West's Key No. Digests, Contracts ☞ 19. (95k19)

b. Revocation by Publication

If a public offer has been made, e.g., in a newspaper, the revocation must be made in the same manner, or by the best means available to reach the same audience.

West's Key No. Digests, Contracts ☞ 19. (95k19)

c. Revocation by Rejection

An offeree's rejection of the offer will normally terminate the offer. A rejection is effective when it has been properly communicated to the offeror or his or her agent.

West's Key No. Digests, Contracts ☞ 21. (95k21)

d. Counteroffers and Confusing Responses

A counteroffer terminates an offer, unless the parties agree otherwise. Under the common law (contracts not covered by the UCC), a conditional acceptance with added terms is also a rejection. However, as will be discussed below, a different result is reached under the UCC. A counter inquiry, a comment on the offer, or a grumbling acceptance do not terminate an offer.

West's Key No. Digests, Contracts ☞ 22, 24. (95k22, 95k24)

> **EXAMPLES:** (1) A student says to a friend: "I'll sell you my old sports car on Friday for $400." The friend says: "I will pay you $300." The *counteroffer* terminates the original offer.
>   (2) A student says to a friend: "I'll sell you my old sports car on Friday for $400." The friend says: "I will pay you $400 if you have it painted first." The *added terms* terminate the original offer.
>   (3) A student says to a friend: "I'll sell you my old sports car on Friday for $400." The friend says: "Would you take $350?" The *inquiry* does not terminate the original offer, which is still open.
>   (4) A student says to a friend: "I'll sell you my old sports car on Friday for $400." The friend says: "That's a lot of money." The *comment* does not terminate the original offer, which is still open.

> (5) A student says to a friend: "I'll sell you my old sports car on Friday for $400." The friend says: "It's highway robbery, but I'll take it." The *grumbling acceptance* does not terminate the original offer, but accepts it.

e. Irrevocable Explicit Option Contracts

Option contracts really consist of two separate agreements. There is an underlying potential contract. Then there is the option feature, which is a separate contract buying the right to accept the underlying contract for a limited period of time. If the offeree gives consideration for the offeror's promise to hold open the offer (for the underlying contract), the offer may not be terminated during the option period.

> **EXAMPLE:** Joseph offered to sell his landscaping business to Tom for $500,000. This was the underlying contract offer. Tom knew that it was a potentially lucrative opportunity, but he wasn't yet ready to go into business. Needing time to consider the offer, Tom paid Joseph $1,000 for an option on the same terms, to be open for 30 days. This was the option contract. The offer to sell the business was then irrevocable for 30 days.

West's Key No. Digests, Sales ☞ 24, 25. (343k24, 343k25)

f. Irrevocable Equitable Option Contracts

If an offeror should know that the offeree, in reliance on an offer, will incur expenses before a formal acceptance can be made, and the offeree does rely, the offer is made irrevocable by law for a reasonable time.

The offeror cannot pull the rug out from under the offeree by withdrawing the offer before the offeree has a chance to accept.

> **EXAMPLE:** A contractor solicits bids from subcontractors for a construction project, so that the contractor can figure her bid to get the job. The contractor then relies on the bids of the subcontractors to determine the overall bid offered to the potential customer. The subcontractors' bids are option contracts, irrevocable for a reasonable time.

g. Irrevocable Merchant's Firm Offer

The UCC provides that a written, signed offer by a merchant to buy or sell goods is irrevocable by law for the time stated or, if no time is stated, for a reasonable time, up to three months (UCC § 2-205).

West's Key No. Digests, Sales ☞ 22(1, 2). (343k22(1), 343k22(2))

h. Irrevocable Offer for Unilateral Contract

A unilateral contract offer cannot be revoked for a reasonable time if the offeree has started performance of the requested act, though performance must be completed before the offeror is under a duty to perform (R2d § 45).

If the offeror hinders performance by the offeree, the offeree is deemed to have begun. An offeree must notify the offeror of performance if the offeror requested it or cannot tell if performance has begun.

> **CASEBOOK EXAMPLE:** *Brackenberry v. Hodgkin,* 116 Me. 399 (1917)
> Mother offered to leave the family farm to her daughter if she and her husband left their home in Missouri and moved to Maine to take care of Mother for the rest of her life. A few weeks after the move, Mother tried to revoke the offer and deed the house to her son. The daughter sued, and the court ruled that the offer was irrevocable since performance had begun.

> **EXAMPLE:** Mother offered to leave the family farm to her daughter if she and her husband left their home in Missouri and moved to Maine to take care of Mother for the rest of her life. Mother refused to let the daughter and family in the house once they moved to Maine. A court would probably rule that the offer was irrevocable since the offeror, Mother, hindered performance.

G. RECOVERY FOR PREPARATION EXPENSES

An offer to form a unilateral contract asks only for an action in return. This may understandably cause an offeree to make preparations to perform in order to accept the offer. An offeree who makes such preparations would be penalized if the offeror then withdrew the offer before the offeree could begin performance. In that case, recovery for those expenses is possible, if the expenses were predictable (*foreseeable*) (R2d § 87(2)).

> **EXAMPLE:** Mother offered to leave the family farm to her daughter if she left their home in Missouri, and moved to Maine to take care of Mother. Then Mother telegraphed the daughter and told her the deal was off, but only after the daughter hired and paid movers to pack all her belongings. A court would probably rule that the daughter can recover the moving expenses she incurred in preparing to respond to her Mother's offer.

II. Acceptance of an Offer

> **OVERVIEW:**
> Acceptance is the procedure used by an offeree to agree to a contract offer. This *manifestation of agreement* must conform to the method required by the offer.

The process of acceptance varies, depending on whether the contract was bilateral, unilateral, or covered by the UCC. Some acceptances must be in writing, if required by the Statute of Frauds, p. 149, **Appendix B: Glossary**.

If an offer is ambiguous as to whether it requires a return promise, as in a bilateral contract, or a return performance, as in a unilateral contract, most courts consider it to be bilateral.

A. BILATERAL CONTRACT ACCEPTANCE

When an offer requests a promise in return, it is a bilateral contract, and the offeree's return promise is required to accept the offer and form a contract. Acceptance can be either written or spoken.

West's Key No. Digests, Contracts ☞ 22. (95k22)

■ 1. Who Can Accept

An offer is personal to an identified offeree, and cannot be assigned to another. Only the offeree may accept the offer, except in the case of option contracts.

> **EXAMPLE:** Ashley sends a fax to cousin Beth: "Beth, I will sell you my sapphire ring for $150." Carol, Beth's roommate, sees the fax and responds: "Beth is not here, but I accept your offer and will buy the ring." There is no contract, because the ability to accept (*power of acceptance*) was limited to Beth.

■ 2. Acceptance Mirrors Offer

Under the common law, the *mirror image rule* requires a valid acceptance to be unqualified and not at variance with the terms of the offer. Any supposed acceptance that adds qualifications or conditions operates as a rejection and a counteroffer.

The UCC is more tolerant of mismatched offers and acceptances, and attempts to reconcile them. It prefers to allow a contract to be formed, rather than conclude that a mismatch is a rejection (see p. 39, **4. The Battle of Forms**).

> **EXAMPLE:** A homeowner sent a contract offer to a house painter, offering to pay $2,000 to have the exterior of his house painted with a specific brand of paint. The painter wrote back, agreeing to most of the terms, except that he wanted to use a different kind of paint. Under the common law, the painter's letter is not an acceptance of the original offer, but a rejection and counteroffer.

■ 3. Objective Commitment

An acceptance is judged by the same standard as an offer.

The test is whether a reasonable person would objectively interpret the words or actions of the offeree as a manifestation of present willingness to accept the offer and enter into a contract.

■ 4. Method of Acceptance

The offeror is master of the offer, and can specify the time, place, or manner of acceptance. If the offer does not specify the manner of acceptance, an offeree may accept in any reasonable manner that communicates the acceptance to the offeror (R2d § 30(2)). To be reasonable, the method of acceptance must be as fast and dependable as the way the offer was presented.

■ 5. Time of Acceptance and the Mailbox Rule

Two common acceptance issues are:

- First, when is an acceptance or a rejection effective?
- Second, what happens when an offeree changes his or her mind?

After originally accepting or rejecting the contract, the *mailbox rule* regulates the winner between conflicting acceptances and rejections, based upon when they have been dispatched to the U.S. Postal Service.

a. Acceptances Are Effective When Dispatched

If an acceptance is properly addressed and stamped, the acceptance will be effective upon dispatch, regardless of whether it ever reaches the offeror.

> **CASEBOOK EXAMPLE:** *Morrison v. Thoelke,* **155 So. 2d 889 (Fla. Ct. App. 1963)**
> A person signed a contract to make a purchase, and sent it to the seller. The seller signed it and mailed it back to the purchaser. The seller then had a change of heart and called the purchaser to revoke the acceptance. Although the attempted revocation by phone reached the purchaser first, once the signed contract was in the mail, the seller had accepted the offer and could not revoke it.

1) Option Contract Exception

The mailbox rule does not apply when the acceptance is for a contract on which the offeree has an option. In that situation, receipt of the acceptance by the offeror is required.

> **EXAMPLE:** A purchases an option for $1,000, giving him the right to purchase B's house for $100,000 for 90 days. If during the option period, A decides to accept and purchase the house, the acceptance is not valid until received by B.

2) Offer's Terms Exception
The mailbox rule does not apply if an offer clearly states otherwise.

b. Rejections Are Effective When Received
If a rejection is sent, it is effective only when it is received by the offeror.

West's Key No. Digests, Contracts ☞ 21. (95k21)

1) Rejection, Then Acceptance
If the offeree first sends a rejection and then an acceptance the rule is: whichever the offeror receives first, wins. The acceptance, if received second, then serves as a counteroffer.

2) Acceptance, Then Rejection, with Reliance
A contract *is* created upon dispatch when an offeree first sends an acceptance, and then sends a rejection, unless the offeror receives the rejection first *and* acts in reliance on it. This is necessary because otherwise the offeror would be penalized for understandably relying on the rejection.

■ 6. Acceptance by Conduct
An offer can be accepted by conduct which implies a return promise, as sought by the offer. It creates a contract as valid as a written one.

West's Key No. Digests, Contracts ☞ 22(1). (95k22(1))

a. Performance
If the offeree begins to perform the act requested by the offeror, this implies a promise to complete the performance and constitutes acceptance.

> **CASEBOOK EXAMPLE:** *Allied Steel v. Ford Motor Co.*, 277 F.2d 907 (1960)
> Ford Motor Co. sent a purchase offer to Allied Steel to buy machinery. Allied, instead of sending back a written acceptance to Ford, directly started to ship the machinery. The shipment constituted an acceptance, and a valid contract was formed.

b. Act Required by the Offer
A unilateral contract requests the performance of an act. A bilateral contract requests a promise to act in the future. A bilateral contract offer can also request an act, not as performance, but to show acceptance.

> **EXAMPLE:** A music studio owner made an offer to a singer: "Our studio will record and mix your next CD for $1,000. This offer can only be accepted by meeting me for lunch on Friday at the Blue Note Cafe." If the singer shows, a contract is formed.

c. Silence

An offer cannot transform the absence of a reply into an acceptance. In other words, an offeror cannot construe silence as consent. However, parties are free to agree beforehand that silence will serve as acceptance. Silence can also be acceptance when the parties' previous *course of dealing* makes it reasonable to require the offeree to give notice of rejection of the offer (R2d § 69(1)(c)).

> **EXAMPLES:** (1) A student received an unsolicited book from a book club. An accompanying letter stated that if the recipient did not send a written refusal to the book club within ten days, the book would be considered accepted and payment would be required. The student can dispose of the book as desired, and need not pay anything. The student's silence does not form a contract because he did not induce the offer.
>
> (2) Another student received an unsolicited book from a book club. The student sent in payment, but signed no other agreement. Books continued to arrive every month, and the student paid for them. One month, the student stopped paying, but still received several more books. Eventually the club stopped sending books and demanded payment. The student claimed that he could keep the free books without paying, since he never requested them. However, the previous course of dealing between the parties makes it reasonable to construe the student's later silence as acceptance. A court probably would conclude that a contract was formed, and he will have to pay for all the books.

d. Accepting Benefits

In most states, acceptance of benefits of unsolicited goods creates an implied contract promise to pay for them.

> **EXAMPLE:** A sends B a set of kitchen knives, offering to sell them to B for $50. B uses the knives for a year. The court probably would find that B's acceptance of benefits created an implied contract.

■ 7. Joint Offers

An offer made jointly to two or more persons must be unanimously accepted to form a contract.

■ 8. Divisible Contracts

Accepting an offer for a divisible series of contracts is different from the all-or-nothing pattern of an ordinary contract. When a contract requires more than one acceptance, this allows the offeror to revoke the offer for the unperformed segments of the contract, even after one in the series has been accepted and fully performed.

> **EXAMPLE:** A supplier made an offer to a farmer: "Our firm will provide you with whatever fertilizer you need for the next 12 months, if our inventory is adequate." The farmer later purchased, paid for, and picked up fertilizer on several occasions. In other words, some segments of the series of contracts were fully performed. However, the supplier can still revoke the offer for the remaining segments in the series of contracts.

B. UNILATERAL CONTRACT ACCEPTANCE

An offer to form a unilateral contract can be accepted only by performance of the act requested in the offer.

Normally, the offeree need not give the offeror notice of an intention to accept.

> **NOTE—*Divergent Notice Distinction:*** If the offeror has no adequate means of learning of the performance, the offeror is not bound to perform unless:
>
> - the offeree uses reasonable diligence to notify the offeror;
> - the offeror learns of performance within a reasonable time; or
> - the offer indicates that notification is unnecessary (R2d § 54).

C. ACCEPTANCE UNDER THE UCC

The UCC attempts to create a contract whenever possible. Thus, it has liberalized the means by which an offeree may accept an offer. Unless the offer expressly limits the manner of acceptance, an offeree may accept in any reasonable manner (UCC § 2-206).

■ 1. Acceptance by Promise

An offeree may accept an offer for the shipment of goods by a promise to ship them (UCC § 2-206).

■ 2. Acceptance by Conforming Shipment

An offeree may accept an offer for the shipment of goods by shipping them. An offeree who ships must notify, within a reasonable time, any offeror who is unaware of the shipment, or the offer will terminate (UCC § 2-206).

West's Key No. Digests, Sales ⟲ 23(3). (343k23(3))

■ 3. Acceptance by Nonconforming Shipment

An offeree may accept by shipping nonconforming goods, simultaneously accepting the offer and breaching the contract. Nonconforming goods are those that do not precisely meet the specifications of the original offer. The buyer can accept the goods if they suit her purposes, reject them if unsuitable, or sue for cover or market value (see p. 85, **PART SEVEN: REMEDIES FOR BREACH**).

However, the offeree can ship nonconforming goods and notify the offeror that the shipment is being offered only as an accommodation to the buyer. The seller's shipment is then a counteroffer. The buyer is free to accept the goods without forming a contract under the terms of the original offer (UCC § 2-206).

West's Key No. Digests, Sales ⟸ 23(3). (343k23(3))

■ 4. The Battle of Forms

In commercial transactions, the UCC addresses the business reality that there are often several inconsistent documents exchanged in creating a sales contract. One party starts by sending an offer to another. The second party might accept the offer, but add a new term. The first party might accept the new term or reject it. The UCC rules dealing with such situations, commonly referred to as the "battle of the forms" provisions, change the common law "mirror-image rule." A battle of the forms can raise two issues:

1. Do the written communications create a contract?

2. If so, what are the terms of the contract?

The applicable UCC provisions are different, depending on whether both parties are merchants.

West's Key No. Digests, Contracts ⟸ 22-24; Sales ⟸ 22(3, 4), 23(3, 4). (95k22 to 95k24, 343k22(3), 343k22(4), 343k23(3), 343k23(4))

a. One Party Is Not a Merchant

If either or both parties to the transaction is not a merchant, and the offeree accepts the offer but, at the same time, adds or changes any terms, the new terms are disregarded and there is a contract under the terms of the original offer. The offeree can always reject the offer and make a counteroffer; he cannot both accept and attempt to add new terms.

> **EXAMPLE:** A student mails an order to Cozy Home Co., for a home repair manual. Cozy sends an acceptance which also says that the student must sign up for woodworking classes. The added term in Cozy's acceptance is only a proposal. There is still a contract, even if the student ignores the classes.

b. Both Parties Are Merchants

If both parties to the transaction are merchants and the offeree accepts the offer but, at the same time, adds or changes nonmaterial terms, the new terms become a part of the contract *unless* the offeree objects within a reasonable time or the original offeror limited acceptance to its own terms. If the new terms *materially* alter the contract, they are disregarded and there is a contract under the terms of the original offer. In general, a term will be considered *material* if it would result in material surprise or hardship, affects warranty rights, or affects the usual remedy for breach (UCC § 2-207(2)).

> **EXAMPLE:** A store owner orders 100 widgets from the supplier. The supplier accepts the offer but adds a term that any disputes as to the quality of the widgets must be submitted to arbitrators. The new term would be considered a material term and would be disregarded. There is a contract under the terms of the original offer.

■ 5. True Counteroffers (The Knock-Out Rule)

If acceptance is expressly made conditional on the offeror's consent to additional or different terms, it is a counteroffer and there is no contract formed (UCC § 2-207). Typical language used in express conditions include "but only if," or "on the condition that," or "provided that."

> **EXAMPLE:** A store ordered carpet from its distributor. The distributor's responding letter agreed to ship the carpet, but specified that it was only "on the condition that any disputes over the contract be submitted to arbitration." The letter is a counteroffer, rejecting the original offer and proposing another.

West's Key No. Digests, Contracts ☞ 24. (95k24)

III. Consideration

> **OVERVIEW:**
> Consideration is the influence which induces a party to enter into a contract. It is a right or benefit accruing to one party, or a loss or responsibility shouldered by the other. Contracts must contain such a benefit for all parties in order to be valid. This mutual consideration is required in addition to the parties' reciprocal promises. Otherwise any agreement is really a gratuitous promise. There may be many distinct promises in a contract. The contract is valid as long as even one promise is supported by consideration.

A. THREE TESTS FOR VALID CONSIDERATION

- The promisor must offer to suffer legal detriment.
- The promise must be made in exchange for a current promise.
- The promise must be obligatory, not discretionary or illusory.

■ 1. Legal Detriment

The one making the promise (the *promisor*) must offer to suffer legal detriment. This means doing something the promisor does not already have a legal obligation to do; or refraining from doing something the promisor has a good faith belief in having the right to do.

> **EXAMPLE:** An uncle offered to pay his nephew $5,000 if the nephew refrained from smoking, drinking, and gambling until 21. The nephew complied, having a good faith, though erroneous, belief that smoking, drinking, and gambling were legal before age 21. The nephew's good faith, though mistaken, forbearance was valid consideration.

West's Key No. Digests, Contracts ☞ 52. (95k52)

a. Noneconomic

A legal detriment can be noneconomic. The benefit sought can be entirely subjective and less tangible.

> **CASEBOOK EXAMPLE:** *Hamer v. Sidway,* 27 N.E. 256 (N.Y. 1891)
> An uncle offered to pay his nephew $5,000 if the nephew refrained from smoking, drinking, and gambling until 21. Smoking, drinking, and gambling were legal before age 21. The nephew complied, and his forbearance was valid consideration.

b. Adequacy

Regardless of how economically inadequate detriment is, it will usually support a promise. Courts usually decline to relieve a party from a contract's terms simply because of making a bad bargain, unless the court finds the bargain unconscionable.

An unconscionable contract is one only a coerced or deluded person would make, and which no honest and fair person would accept, because the terms are excessively extreme and one-sided.

West's Key No. Digests, Contracts ☞ 53. (95k53)

c. Nominal Consideration

Contracts often recite nominal or token consideration such as "in consideration of $1 paid." A court may conclude that consideration has not been paid, or that the parties intended a gift rather than a contract.

> **EXAMPLE:** A father signed a contract transferring all his household furniture to his daughter, in return for one dollar. The daughter did not take possession of the furniture. After the father's death, the daughter was unable to enforce the contract to receive the furniture. The court ruled that the supposed transfer was no more than a failed gift because there was no valid consideration.

d. The Preexisting Duty Rule

If a party is currently legally obligated to do something, or is prohibited from doing it, she has a *preexisting duty*. If she then promises to do or hold back from doing the same thing, she has not incurred any new detriment. The same is true if she then actually does or holds back from doing the thing. Accordingly, the promise or act is not good consideration (R2d § 73). However, there are two common law exceptions to the rule, and the UCC has abolished it entirely for sales of goods (UCC § 2-209).

> **EXAMPLE:** A homeowner contracted with a house painter to have the exterior of his house painted for $2,000. The painter later decided he wanted $2,500, and the homeowner agreed. After the job was completed, the painter could not recover the extra $500 from the second agreement. Since the painter already had a preexisting duty to paint the house, his second agreement to paint it lacked any new consideration.

West's Key No. Digests, Contracts ☞ 67. (95k67)

1) Accord and Satisfaction Exception

A party can use a preexisting duty as the basis for an accord and satisfaction. Accord and satisfaction is a procedure for resolving contract disputes through compromise. One party offers a compromise to fulfill (*discharge*) an existing debt or duty. The new, compromise agreement is called the *accord*. The *satisfaction* is the actual performance of the agreement, which discharges both the old and new obligations.

> **CASEBOOK EXAMPLE:** *Cohen v. Sabin*, 452 Pa. 447, 307 A.2d 845 (1973)
> A union official retired with a pension. In negotiating the disputed pension rate, the union and the official agreed to base it on his after-tax annual salary of $25,000 (that is the accord). The official received payments for two years (that is the satisfaction). The official then sued, claiming the pension should have been based on his pretax salary of $41,000, which would have increased the pension. The court held that the plaintiff's acceptance of the pension payments constituted an accord and satisfaction of the disputed obligation, and prevented (*estopped*) him from seeking an increase.

2) Minority Rule Benefits Exception

In some jurisdictions, the preexisting duty rule is not applied if the promisee owes the preexisting duty to a third person. Thus a person already under contract to perform a particular task can enter into a second contract with a different person to perform the same task.

> **EXAMPLE:** Jake agreed to landscape Dorothy's yard by May 1. Dorothy's neighbor, Ms. Gulch, planning a wedding in her yard on May 8, offered Jake an additional $100 to ensure completion on time, and he accepted. Though Jake's second promise had no added legal detriment, Ms. Gulch was benefitted and must pay the $100.

■ 2. Exchange of Current Promise or Performance

The promise must be made in exchange for the promisee's *current* exchange of a promise or performance. This is often referred to as a "bargained-for exchange." The key idea is that the promise is for a present promise or performance, not a past or future one.

West's Key No. Digests, Contracts ☞ 55. (95k55)

a. Past Performance Usually Invalid

The promisor must request and induce the promisee's forthcoming or current detriment in exchange for the promise. There has to be an exchange of current promises to do something in the future, or refrain from something. This is called a *bargained-for exchange.*

If a promisor makes a promise in return for something already done (*past performance*), there is usually no consideration, and no contract, with a few exceptions.

> **EXAMPLE:** The boss asked his secretary to work late. The secretary stayed. As a result, the boss promised to pay the secretary a bonus. The boss's promise is unenforceable, because the secretary already performed the work and thus the promise does not induce him to bargain to do anything in exchange.

1) Revived Debt Exception

When a debt is no longer legally enforceable, for example, because of bankruptcy, if the debtor promises to repay all or part of the debt, the new promise to pay is enforceable on the new terms.

2) Reaffirmed Contract Exception

A party may form a contract which he has the power to void. For example, a contract with an infant (anyone under 18) can usually be voided by the infant. After age 18, the party can ratify the contract. If he reaffirms a promise that he has the power to void, the subsequent promise to perform is enforceable without added consideration.

3) Induced Past Performance Exception

If a person performs an act at the request of another with an expectation of payment, courts may enforce a later promise to pay proportionate to the benefit received (R2d § 86(2)(b)).

> **EXAMPLE:** The boss asked his secretary to work late one evening. Because the secretary knew that the boss always paid secretaries who stay late an extra $100, he stayed and finished the project. The next morning, the boss promised to pay him $100 because he stayed late the night before. The boss's promise is enforceable, because the secretary was induced to perform by the expected bonus.

b. Moral Consideration Invalid

If a promisor makes a promise because of feeling a moral obligation, the promise does not induce a current exchange of performance from the promisee and lacks consideration.

> **EXAMPLE:** Joe tells his brother Tom, "Since you named your son after me, I promise to leave you my yacht." This promise is unenforceable for lack of consideration.

West's Key No. Digests, Contracts ⚷ 76. (95k76)

c. Gratuitous Promises for Gifts

A promise to make a gift is unenforceable because it is unsupported by consideration and the promisee suffers no legal detriment. A conditional gift also lacks consideration if there was no bargain between the parties, even if the promisee suffers a detriment.

> **CASEBOOK EXAMPLE:** *Kirksey v. Kirksey*, 8 Ala. 131 (1845)
> A man asked his widowed sister-in-law to move across state with her kids and stay with him. She gave up her home and moved. He kicked her out a few years later. The court ruled there was no consideration.

When an agreement is both a gift and a negotiated business transaction, there can still be valid consideration and contract formation. The bargain simply has to be induced at least partially by the benefits of the deal, as opposed to being completely motivated by the altruism of gift-giving.

> **EXAMPLE:** Joni agrees to sell her old sports car to her good friend, Carla, for $300 rather than the $400 she would ask from a stranger. The generous or gift-giving aspect of the sale does not invalidate the consideration, and there is a still a valid contract.

■ 3. Obligatory, Not Illusory

A promise must be binding and obligatory in order to be considered adequate consideration. The power to revoke the contract cannot be reserved by one party. If the promisor has complete discretion on whether to perform, the promise is illusory and unenforceable, because it is no promise at all.

> **EXAMPLE:** A creditor said to a debtor: "I'll refrain from collecting on your debt until I need the money, if you promise to purchase my old sports car from me." The creditor made no commitment. The promise and the contract are illusory.

a. Mutuality

In bilateral contracts, a promise constitutes consideration for the return promise only if both parties are bound to perform. Without mutuality of obligation, the contract is void. In unilateral contracts, since acceptance occurs only upon performance of an act, the act is the consideration.

West's Key No. Digests, Contracts ☞ 57. (95k57)

b. Alternative Performances

If a promisor reserves a number of alternative performances, they constitute consideration *only if each one* involves legal detriment to the promisor, or if the choice among alternatives rests with a third party not under the promisor's control (R2d § 77(b)). There cannot be an escape hatch for the promisor.

> **EXAMPLE:** The hiring partner of a law firm says to an attorney: "If Netscape retains the firm, we will either hire you next month or we will put you on a list for further consideration." The second promise bears no cost or detriment for the firm and is not good consideration. There is no contract.

c. Conditioned Promises

A conditional promise can constitute valid consideration, but only if the condition is entirely outside of the promisor's control.

> **EXAMPLES:** (1) The hiring partner of a law firm says to an attorney: "We will hire you if we get Netscape as a client next month." If Netscape retains the firm, the consideration and contract are valid.
> (2) The hiring partner of a law firm says to an attorney: "We will hire you if we decide to expand the firm next month." Since the decision to expand is controlled

> by the firm, it made no binding commitment. There is no consideration and no contract.

West's Key No. Digests, Contracts ☞ 58. (95k58)

d. Satisfied Promisor

If a party agrees to perform only if satisfied with the goods or services bargained for, that party has a good faith obligation to accept the goods or services if actually satisfied, and this constitutes good consideration.

e. Implied Promises

An apparently illusory promise may be rendered sufficient consideration if a court finds an implied promise to use one's best efforts to perform.

The promise is a sufficient legal detriment, rendering the contract binding. An agreement giving an exclusive right to sell goods imposes by law an obligation to use best efforts (UCC § 2-306(2)).

> **CASEBOOK EXAMPLE:** *Wood v. Lucy, Lady Duff Gordon,* **222 N.Y. 88 (1917)**
> Lucy contracted to market her clothing line exclusively through Mr. Wood, for a 50–50 share of the profits. Later she resold the rights, arguing that there was no consideration and no contract, because Wood had no duty to sell anything specific. The court ruled in favor of Wood, finding there was a promise implied by him to try in good faith to sell the clothes. The implied promise was sufficient consideration to make the contract binding.

f. Restricted Cancellation

An absolute right to cancel an agreement makes the promises contained in the agreement "illusory" as the promisor does not have to perform. But if the right to cancel is restricted, the promise contained in the contract may still constitute good consideration. For example, a clause stating "Seller may terminate only upon 30 days' notice" is a limitation on the seller's right to cancel and the restricted cancellation clause will not make the contract illusory.

> **EXAMPLES:** (1) A painter contracts with a supplier to purchase ten gallons of paint every month. The agreement states that the painter may cancel the arrangement at any time. Because the painter made no binding commitment, there is no consideration and no contract.
>
> (2) A painter contracts with a supplier to purchase ten gallons of paint every month. The agreement states that the painter may cancel the arrangement only after 30 days' notice. There is good consideration and a contract.

Under the UCC, an unrestricted cancellation clause will not make the contract illusory. The UCC requires all parties to exercise "good faith" in invoking a cancellation clause and therefore, all cancellation clauses are in a sense "restricted."

g. Unenforceable by Law

The fact that a rule of law renders a promise voidable or unenforceable does not prevent it from being consideration. This can be important, if the contract later becomes enforceable through performance or conduct of the parties.

> **EXAMPLE:** Buyer orally promised to purchase $600 worth of paint from Seller. The Statute of Frauds rendered Buyer's promise and the contract unenforceable. The promise still constitutes consideration. If the seller delivered the paint and the buyer accepted it, the parties' conduct would make the contract enforceable.

West's Key No. Digests, Contracts ☞ 81. (95k81)

h. Requirements and Output Contracts

Contracts made to purchase all of one's requirements or to sell all of one's output are not illusory. Each party must in good faith tender or demand any amount of goods not unreasonably disproportionate to any estimate or comparable output or requirements (UCC § 2-306).

> **EXAMPLES:** (1) A builder contracts with a distributor to purchase all the lumber she needs that year for home building. Even though a specific amount is not stated, it is a valid requirements contract.
>
> (2) A saw mill contracts with a home builder to provide all the lumber it can produce this year. Even though a specific amount is not stated, it is a valid output contract. However, if the saw mill decided to increase output by ten times over the previous year, the amount would be disproportionate and the contract invalid.

West's Key No. Digests, Sales ☞ 19. (343k19)

B. CONSIDERATION SUBSTITUTES

Certain promises are at least partially enforceable, even without an exchange of true consideration. There are several substitutes for consideration, used when justice and custom require it.

■ 1. Common Law Substitutes

a. Promissory Estoppel

The principle of promissory estoppel is applied when there has been a promise which the promisor should reasonably expect to induce action or forbearance on the part of the promisee, and which did induce such action or forbearance. Such a promise is binding if injustice can be avoided only by enforcement of the promise.

> **CASEBOOK EXAMPLE:** *Feinberg v. Pfeiffer Co.*, 322 S.W.2d 163 (Mo. Ct. App. 1959) Mrs. Feinberg worked for Pfeiffer Co. for 37 years. The company told her they would give her a pension of $200 a month if she retired, which she did. The company later cut the pension to $100 per month, and she sued. Even though the pension was a gratuitous gift, the court held that she detrimentally, reasonably, and foreseeably relied on it, and it was enforceable.

West's Key No. Digests, Estoppel ⊕ 85. (156k85)

b. Minority Rule—Option Contracts
Some courts do not require consideration for formation of an option contract, holding that the contract is binding if it is in writing, is signed by the offeror, recites a supposed consideration for making the offer, and proposes a fair exchange within a reasonable time (R2d § 87(1)).

c. Archaic—Contracts under Seal
Historically, at common law, a contract made under seal, i.e., an impression formed in melted wax on parchment, did not require consideration to be enforceable after delivery of the sealed instrument.

■ 2. UCC Substitutes

a. Merchants' Firm Offers
A written offer by a merchant to buy or sell goods, that gives assurance that it will be held open, is not revocable for lack of consideration, during the time stated or, if no time is stated, for a reasonable time, not to exceed three months.

b. Contract Modifications
If contracting parties, in good faith, modify a contract for the sale of goods, no added consideration is needed. The UCC has essentially abolished the preexisting duty rule in these cases (UCC § 2-209).

c. Waiver
If contracting parties, in good faith, waive aspects of a contract for the sale of goods, no added consideration is needed (UCC § 2-209).

PART THREE: INTERPRETATION

OVERVIEW:

Contracts must be interpreted, because different legal principles sometimes control different types of contracts. The intent of the contracting parties is the most important factor in categorizing a contract, but if a contract is unclear, the law often intervenes. The quest is to determine what the meaning of the contract really is.

Interpretation of an unambiguous contract is always done by a court. On the other hand, when a contract is ambiguous, it is the responsibility of the jury to resolve any ambiguities. One limitation on the evidence which can be used to resolve contract disputes is the parol evidence rule, discussed below. This limits the contract to its terms, and tries to exclude other extraneous evidence.

I. Types of Contracts

A. EXPRESS CONTRACT

An express contract can be either a written or an oral agreement. It is the actual agreement of the parties, the terms of which are openly uttered or declared at the time of making it, being stated in distinct and explicit language, either orally or in writing.

> **EXAMPLE:** A student says to a classmate: "I'll sell you my old sports car for $400," and the classmate says: "I accept." They draw up and sign an agreement. That is an *express* contract.

West's Key No. Digests, Contracts ⟲ 3. (95k3)

B. IMPLIED CONTRACT

An implied contract is one in which the terms of the agreement are not clearly stated, but may be inferred from the parties' conduct.

If one or both parties accept the benefits of the other's performance without objection, a contract is implied. Under the UCC, contracts may also be established from the course of dealing, trade usage, or course of performance (UCC § 1-205(1)).

> **EXAMPLE:** A patron says to a waiter: "I want the spaghetti marinara." This is the acceptance of an *implied* contract offer. The patron's promise to pay the menu price is implied.

West's Key No. Digests, Contracts ☞ 27. (95k27)

C. QUASI CONTRACTS

This is a type of contract created by law when necessary to avoid unjust enrichment.

It is designed to compensate a party for the reasonable value of services or costs of performance when there is no actual contract.

> **EXAMPLE:** A bleeding person rushes to a hospital and is treated. The patient's conduct creates a *quasi* contract. The patient must pay for the treatment, even though there is no formal contract.

West's Key No. Digests, Implied and Constructive Contracts ☞ 2. (205Hk2)

D. DIVISIBLE OR ENTIRE

Some contracts are divisible into independent acts, each of which confers a separate benefit, and for which a separate payment is deserved.

These are divisible contracts. In those cases, performance of each separate act triggers the payment of consideration.

> **EXAMPLE:** A student says to a classmate: "I'll make you dinner each Friday this winter, for $20 per meal," and the classmate says: "I accept." Payment is due after each meal, not in the spring.

Other contracts are entire or nondivisible. In this case, only substantial completion or performance of the entire contract triggers the payment of consideration.

> **EXAMPLE:** A student says to a classmate: "I'll cater your graduation dinner on Friday for $200," and the classmate says: "I accept." Payment is due only after the entire meal, not after one course.

West's Key No. Digests, Contracts ☞ 171. (95k171)

E. BILATERAL CONTRACTS

A bilateral contract is formed when two parties exchange mutually dependent promises. When the promises are exchanged, the contract is formed even though the promises are fulfilled later.

West's Key No. Digests, Contracts ☞ 10(1). (95k10(1))

F. UNILATERAL CONTRACTS

A unilateral contract is formed when one party offers to perform and requests a return performance—not a promise.

The second party can *only* accept by performing. The offeror must make it clear that the contract is formed only upon the offeree's performance. In case of doubt, courts will presume that an offer invites only a promise, as in the formation of a bilateral contract.

> **EXAMPLE:** A student says to a friend: "I'll pay you $20 if you make me dinner this Friday." The student-offeror is not asking for a promise, but for a meal. The friend can ignore the offer, but can accept it only by actually making the dinner. Even if the friend says "I promise to make the meal on Friday," there is still no contract until the food is served. A contract is formed by the beginning of performance, so that once the friend is cooking, the student cannot withdraw the offer.

West's Key No. Digests, Contracts ☞ 10(1). (95k10(1))

G. UCC

The distinction between bilateral and unilateral contracts is not true for transactions covered by the UCC. The UCC, designed to advance the cause of commerce, wants to encourage contracts. Accordingly, it allows acceptance by either performance or a return promise, unless the parties specify otherwise (UCC § 2-206(b)).

II. The Parol Evidence Rule

OVERVIEW:
The rule is used when one party to a contract wants to introduce some evidence that is not found in the final, written contract already in existence, and the other party opposes the introduction.

Under the parol evidence rule, if the parties have reduced their agreement to writing which they intend to be final and complete, they cannot contradict it or change it with evidence of prior oral or written or contemporaneous oral agreements.

The rule only applies when there is a final, complete, written contract. If there is only a preliminary draft, or if the contract is ambiguous, the rule does not apply.

There are competing considerations which are reconciled by the rule. On the one hand, it is important to reveal the accurate outline of a contract. On the other hand, the law seeks to avoid spurious claims and untruths. The rule is used because disputes can be thorny if the parties disagree on what terms are included in a contract. In order to avoid the temptation for oral perjury and to avoid unjustified claims, the law excludes certain types of extraneous evidence by this method.

> **EXAMPLE:** A student says to a friend: "I'll sell you my old sports car for $400," and the friend says: "I accept." They draw up and sign a complete, written contract. Later, the friend claims that the student had also agreed by phone to accept an old Ford as a trade-in. The trade-in is not part of the contract.

West's Key No. Digests, Evidence ☞ 384-427. (157XI(A))

A. FINAL CONTRACT
Parol evidence is admissible to show that no final contract exists. The rule does not apply until a final contract is formed.

B. TOTALLY INTEGRATED WRITING
If a written contract includes all essential terms, the document is totally integrated. In that case, a court will not admit evidence of prior or contemporaneous agreements or negotiations which would contradict the writing or add another term to it.

■ 1. Integration Clause and Complete Contract
If the writing contains a clause stating that the agreement is the parties' final and complete agreement—known as a *merger or integration clause*—the writing is totally integrated, unless the document is clearly incomplete. Parol evidence is inadmissible.

> **EXAMPLES:** (1) A typical integration clause: *"This Agreement supersedes all prior agreements between the Parties, it being their intention that this Agreement shall constitute the complete settlement of all their rights and interests of any kind."*
> (2) A buyer orally agreed to purchase the seller's boat. Seller also owns a boat trailer. The parties' written agreement did not mention the trailer. The buyer

has other evidence showing that the seller agreed to "throw in" the trailer to induce the purchase. If the writing contained an integration clause and was otherwise complete, evidence of the seller's promise to include the trailer as part of the sale would be prohibited.

■ 2. Partially Integrated

If there is no integration clause, and additional terms that are normally needed are usually left out in similar circumstances, the writing is considered a partial integration. Parol evidence is not admissible to contradict a term of the writing, but is admissible to prove the existence of omitted, consistent, additional terms.

■ 3. Integration Clause but Incomplete

If there is a merger or integration clause, but the writing is clearly incomplete, it is not a final document. Parol evidence is admissible.

C. UCC AND PAROL EVIDENCE

Under UCC § 2A-202(a), a party may explain or supplement, but not contradict, even a totally integrated writing by offering evidence of the following.

■ 1. Course of Dealing

This is defined as the sequence of previous conduct between the parties in a particular transaction that is regarded as a common basis of understanding for interpreting the parties' expressions.

West's Key No. Digests, Contracts ⬭ 170. (95k170)

■ 2. Usage of Trade

Usage of trade means a regular practice or method of dealing used in the parties' business that gives rise to an expectation that the parties will observe it with respect to the transaction in question.

West's Key No. Digests, Customs and Usages ⬭ 15-17. (113k15 to 113k17)

■ 3. Course of Performance

The definition of course of performance is the manner in which the parties have conducted themselves in performing the particular contract at hand.

West's Key No. Digests, Contracts ⬭ 170. (95k170)

D. PAROL EVIDENCE RULE INAPPLICABLE

■ 1. Clarifying Ambiguity

The parol evidence rule does not apply when a party wants to clarify ambiguous terms. Traditionally, only terms with a special meaning due to custom or usage could be varied, but not the plain meaning of ordinary words. More recently, parties are allowed to introduce parol evidence showing that they attached a special meaning to any word. Ambiguous terms are normally construed against the drafter (UCC § 2-202).

West's Key No. Digests, Evidence ☞ 448-463. (157XI(D))

■ 2. Later Oral or Written Negotiations

The rule does not prevent admission of evidence of later written or oral negotiations, made after a writing has been signed, in order to contradict it.

West's Key No. Digests, Evidence ☞ 439-445. (157XI(C))

■ 3. Separate Contracts

Parol evidence is admissible to prove a collateral contract, distinct from and independent of the written agreement which will not vary or contradict its terms.

West's Key No. Digests, Evidence ☞ 439-445. (157XI(C))

■ 4. Contract Avoidance

When a party seeks to avoid a contract, the parol evidence rule does not apply. For example, a court will admit evidence of fraud, duress, mistake, illegality, incapacity, or misrepresentation.

West's Key No. Digests, Evidence ☞ 428-437. (157XI(B))

■ 5. Conditions Precedent

If the parties orally agreed that no contract would be formed until a particular event occurred, but the writing does not make mention of it, a party can offer other evidence of the condition precedent agreement.

West's Key No. Digests, Evidence ☞ 420. (157k420)

■ **6. Failure of Consideration**

The parol evidence rule will not prevent a party from showing absence of consideration. A party may contradict the writing's recital of consideration with extrinsic evidence.

West's Key No. Digests, Evidence ☞ 432. (157k432)

PART FOUR: DEFENSES

OVERVIEW:
Even if it appears that a valid contract has been formed, if a party has a *defense* to formation or enforcement, no duties or rights are operative. Defenses serve many important public policies, such as the avoidance of fraud or excessively unfair contracts, and the protection of parties without the mental ability to understand the nature of the agreements they are making.

There are formation and public policy defenses, and an enforcement defense. *Formation defenses* include missing elements, mistake, nonexistence of subject matter, incapacity, fraud and misrepresentation, and undue influence. *Public policy defenses* include illegality and unconscionability. The *enforcement defense* is based on the Statute of Frauds. This requires tangible written evidence to prove that a contract was made.

It is important to understand the type of defense being advanced, because the consequences vary, creating void contracts which are no contract at all; voidable contracts, which are valid but can be revoked; and unenforceable contracts, which are valid but cannot be enforced unless there are further developments.

I. Types of Invalid Contracts

A. VOID CONTRACT

A **void contract** is one that could not be formed because of a fatal legal impediment.

It is an agreement that is not a contract at all. Neither party is bound and neither may bring an action against the other for breach. It is void from the beginning, or *ab initio*.

> **EXAMPLE:** A firm signs a written employment contract with an attorney. The attorney has been previously adjudicated by a court to lack mental capacity, although the firm is unaware of that fact. Mental capacity is the ability to understand the nature and extent of a contract. The employment contract is void as though it never existed.

West's Key No. Digests, Contracts ☞ 85, 136. (95k85, 95k136)

B. VOIDABLE CONTRACT

A **voidable contract** is one that was originally valid, but which a party has the optional power to revoke or nullify.

One example is certain agreements made by an adult with a minor, who has the option of backing out of the deal. However, until the contract is voided, it is valid.

West's Key No. Digests, Contracts ☞ 85, 136. (95k85, 95k136)

C. UNENFORCEABLE CONTRACT

An **unenforceable contract** is one which is potentially valid, but which cannot be enforced because it has a defect.

Based on the defect, one party has a defense to enforcement—but the defect can be remedied. Although such a contract cannot be immediately enforced, it has a continuing, latent validity. Parties may later act to cure the defect and render such a contract enforceable.

> **EXAMPLE:** Jim agrees to sell Gordie $750 worth of bird feeders. The contract is unenforceable at that point because under the Statute of Frauds it must be in writing. However, if Gordie then delivers a written purchase order and Jim ships the feeders, such performance cures the defect in the contract and it becomes enforceable.

II. Formation Defenses

A. MISSING ESSENTIAL ELEMENT

If an agreement lacks one essential element, it is not a contract at all.

The absence of a valid offer, acceptance, or consideration makes an agreement noncontractual. Although this is perspicuous, it is often missed on exams, perhaps because it seems too obvious. Always ask this question first: Is it a contract?

West's Key No. Digests, Contracts 🗝 9(1). (95k9(1))

B. MISTAKE DEFENSES

A mistake affects the formation of a contract if it relates to a material fact. Material means necessary to the contract, as opposed to secondary, and having an effect upon the parties. Mistakes may be unilateral, mutual, or due to latent ambiguities. These are some of the most confusing contract issues.

West's Key No. Digests, Contracts 🗝 93. (95k93)

■ 1. Unilateral Mistake

As a general rule, a party cannot get relief for a unilateral mistake. When, however, a party makes a unilateral mistake of a material fact, and the other party knew or should have known of the mistake, the party making the mistake can avoid the contract.

> **EXAMPLES**: (1) The general contractor Patton invited bids from subcontractors for a new building. Franklin inadvertently submitted a bid which was only 10 percent of its true cost. Patton was a veteran contractor and accepted the bid (which is a contract offer). Patton knew that the materials alone exceeded Franklin's bid and the other bids were ten times higher. Franklin can withdraw his bid, because Patton knew or should have known that the bid was in error. There is no contract.
> (2) Bradley invited bids from subcontractors for a new building. Franklin inadvertently submitted a bid which was only 50 percent of its true cost. Bradley was new to the business and accepted the bid (which is a contract offer). Bradley had no way of knowing how low the bid was. Franklin's bid was an offer which formed a valid contract; his mistake is not grounds for revoking (*rescinding*) the contract.

> **NOTE—*Divergent Minority Rule*:** Some courts allow a mistaken party to void a contract even if the other party did not know of the mistake, if enforcement would be oppressive to the mistaken party and would not be a substantial hardship to the other party.
>
> **EXAMPLE:** Patton invited bids from subcontractors for a new building. Franklin submitted a bid which was only 10 percent of its value, due to an error in calculation. Patton was new to the business and had no way of knowing how low

the bid was. Some courts would still allow Franklin to withdraw his bid because it would be too oppressive to him, and Patton would ultimately have to pay only what the job was really worth.

■ 2. Mutual Mistake

If both parties to a contract make a false, affirmative, common assumption about a material issue, no contract is formed because there is no meeting of minds.

West's Key No. Digests, Contracts ☞ 93(5). (95k93(5))

a. Mistake in Quality

Many mistakes relate to the quality of the thing for which the contract was made. The mistake must be so severe an imbalance that it would be unfair to carry it out (R2d § 152, Comment c).

> **CASEBOOK EXAMPLE:** *Sherwood v. Walker,* 33 N.W. 919 (Mich. 1887)
> Two experienced farmers contracted for the sale of a cow, Rose the 2nd of Aberlone, which both judged to be unable to breed. The contract price of $80 was based on that assumption. Rose turned out to be pregnant, and worth about $800. Because both parties had made the same material mistake, there was no contract.

b. Nonexistence of Subject Matter

If the subject matter of the contract does not exist, the parties cannot be held to a contract for its sale. If someone inherits a manuscript and contracts to sell the copyright to a publisher, only to later discover that the manuscript is in the public realm, both parties were mistaken as to the existence of a copyright, and there is no contract.

West's Key No. Digests, Contracts ☞ 8, 93(5). (95k8, 95k93(5))

c. Not Conscious Uncertainty

Mutual mistake must amount to more than a *conscious uncertainty.* A mistake regarding the value of the subject matter of a contract will not justify rescission if the parties assumed the risk of being wrong. In other words, if the parties don't know, don't investigate, and don't care, neither can claim later the defense of mutual mistake. If the parties choose to be ignorant, the law will not intervene to revoke a contract.

> **CASEBOOK EXAMPLE:** *Wood v. Boynton,* 25 N.W. 42 (Wisc. 1885)
> A rock hound took a small, unassuming stone to a jeweler, who thought it might be a topaz, and paid a dollar for it. Neither party knew that it was actually a $700 diamond. Because the parties were mutually unconcerned about the nature of the stone prior to the sale, the court ruled that the contract was valid.

d. UCC Warranty Exception

If both buyer and seller are mistaken as to the nature or quality of goods which are less valuable than assumed, the buyer may bring an action against the seller for breach of warranty and rescission of the contract (UCC § 2-714(2)).

> **EXAMPLE:** A jeweler contracted to buy flawless diamonds from a distributor. The distributor delivered diamonds, not knowing they were inconspicuously flawed. When the jeweler inspected the diamonds and realized the mistake, he could rescind the sale. Alternatively, he could sue for money damages to recover the difference in value between the flawless and flawed diamonds.

West's Key No. Digests, Sales ☞ 262.5. (343k262.5)

■ 3. Latent Ambiguities

If parties have made an agreement, but have subjectively attached different meanings to the terms, those terms are latently ambiguous and no contract is formed.

West's Key No. Digests, Contracts ☞ 9(1); Evidence ☞ 452. (95k9(1), 157k452)

a. If Neither Party Knows

If neither party knew of an ambiguity, i.e., of the different meaning attached by the other at the time the agreement was made, no contract is formed.

> **CASEBOOK EXAMPLE:** *Raffles v. Wichelhaus,* **159 Eng. Rep. 375 (1864)**
> A buyer agreed to buy cotton from a seller, to be transported from India on the ship *Peerless*. The parties later discovered that there were two ships called *Peerless*. The buyer meant the one scheduled to dock in September; the seller meant the one scheduled to dock in December. Since neither party was aware of the meaning of *Peerless* attached by the other, there was no meeting of minds, and no contract was formed.

b. If One Party Knows

If one of the contracting parties knew or should have known the different meaning attached by the other party, a contract is formed and the meaning attached by the innocent party prevails.

> **EXAMPLE:** George contracts to buy Ringo's guitar. Unknown to George, Ringo has two guitars, a valuable Fender and an inexpensive copy. Ringo intends to part with the copy but knows that George thinks he is getting the Fender. The contract is valid but George's interpretation prevails.

c. If Both Parties Know

If both parties knew of a different meaning attached by the other at the time the agreement was made, no contract is formed.

> **EXAMPLE:** A buyer agreed to buy cotton from a seller, to be transported on the ship *Peerless*. There were two ships called *Peerless*. The buyer meant the one scheduled to dock in September; the seller meant the one scheduled to dock in December. *Both parties knew that the other intended a different ship.* No contract was formed.

C. INCAPACITY

Certain classes of persons lack the ordinary capacity to make contracts. Contracts they form are void or voidable, although the contracts can be reaffirmed after the incapacity ends.

■ 1. Infants

Persons under the age of majority (usually 18) are termed *infants*.

Most contracts made by infants are voidable by them or their guardian.

West's Key No. Digests, Infants ☞ 46. (211k46)

a. Third Parties

An infant's right to void a contract is sometimes effective even against a third party. If an infant sold her house, and the buyer sold it to another, the infant could still disaffirm the sale and regain title.

b. UCC

However, under the UCC, if an infant sold goods to a buyer, who then sold them to another who paid for them while unaware of the problem with the earlier sale, the last buyer is *a good faith purchaser for value*. The infant may not recover the goods (UCC § 2-403).

■ 2. Mental Incompetence

West's Key No. Digests, Mental Health ☞ 372. (257Ak372)

a. Adjudicated Incompetent

If a person is adjudicated to lack the mental capacity to understand the nature and consequences of a contract, any contract made by that person is *void* from the beginning.

It does not matter whether the other parties had actual knowledge or notice of the incapacity.

West's Key No. Digests, Mental Health ☞ 374. (257Ak374)

b. Mental Illness, Intoxication, or Senility

If a person who has not been adjudicated incompetent does not understand the nature and consequences of entering into a contract due to mental incapacity, the contract is voidable. Mental illness, intoxication, and senility can create this mental incapacity. However, an afflicted person can void contracts only when the other person knew or should have known of the incapacity. The person or person's legal representative may disaffirm a contract made under these conditions.

■ 3. Necessities

The defense does not apply to contracts for necessities for living, such as food. In addition, contracts made for insurance, banking, student loans, and military enlistments are still enforceable by special statutes.

West's Key No. Digests, Infants ⚖ 50; Mental Health ⚖ 375. (211k50, 257Ak375)

■ 4. Reaffirmation

After reaching the age of majority, or recovering from mental infirmity, a party may affirm the obligations of a voidable contract. Such affirmance may be express, by conduct, or by failure to make a timely disaffirmance within a reasonable time. No further consideration is needed.

> **EXAMPLES:** (1) A 17-year-old contracted to purchase a car from a used car dealer. After he turned 18, he knew he wanted to keep the car, and so he signed a contract reaffirming his original obligation. The new contract is valid and binding.
> (2) A 17-year-old contracted to purchase a car from a used car dealer. He kept the car until he was 20, and then attempted to void the contract. His failure to act sooner made the contract valid and binding.

West's Key No. Digests, Infants ⚖ 57; Mental Health ⚖ 396. (211k57, 257Ak396)

D. FRAUD AND MISREPRESENTATION

When a party has fraudulently induced another to enter into a contract, it is voidable.

If the fraud goes to the heart of the contract, the contract is void from the beginning.

West's Key No. Digests, Contracts ⚖ 94. (95k94)

■ 1. Fraud in Inducement

Fraud in inducement is fraudulently inducing another to enter into a contract by misrepresenting the subject matter of the contract.

This is fraud which somewhat diminishes the value of the bargain, although it does not completely destroy it. It renders a contract voidable by the deceived party; it does not negate the existence of a contract.

> **CASEBOOK EXAMPLE:** *Tyler v. Bennett,* 449 S.E.2d 666 (Ga. Ct. App. 1994)
> Tyler sold his title search company to Bennett. Tyler disclosed that he was being investigated for fraudulently laundering money from his clients, but asserted that he was innocent of all charges. In fact, after selling Bennett the business, Tyler pled guilty to bank fraud. In ensuing litigation, Bennett was awarded damages, based in part upon Bennett's claim that Tyler's deceit was *fraud in inducement,* diminishing the value of the business purchased.

■ **2. Fraud in Factum**

Fraud in factum, or execution, is fraud of such a nature that the deceived party neither knew or should have known of the character or basic terms of the transaction.

This is fraud which is so severe that the innocent party was prevented from understanding the basic nature of the bargain. It renders a contract void from the beginning (R2d § 163).

> **CASEBOOK EXAMPLE:** *Iron Workers' Local No. 25 v. Klassic Services,* 913 F. Supp. 541 (E.D. Michigan 1996)
> An officer of a mining company signed an agreement presented to him by the union. The officer was told the agreement did not contain an obligation to contribute to a union pension fund, when it actually did. Additionally, the union said that the agreement only covered work to be performed for four days, when it actually covered three years. The court initially ruled that proof of these claims would constitute *fraud in the execution,* making the agreement void.

■ **3. Innocent Misrepresentation**

If a party innocently misrepresented a fact, the party seeking to avoid the contract must show that the misrepresentation was material, i.e., likely to affect the conduct of a reasonable person, and that the deceived party relied on it.

> **EXAMPLE:** The sellers of a bakery made misrepresentations as to the zoning of the business location. However, the sellers made the misrepresentations in good faith, having themselves been given erroneous information by the city. Unless the buyers can prove that the zoning was material, and that they relied on it, they cannot rescind the contract for sale.

■ **4. Intentional Misrepresentation**

If the misrepresentation was intentional, actual reliance is all that is necessary and the fact misrepresented need not have been material.

> **EXAMPLE:** The buyers of a bakery claimed that the sellers made misrepresentations as to the zoning of the business. The sellers made the misrepresentations intentionally, having been previously informed by the city as to the proper zoning. If the buyers merely can prove that they relied on the zoning, they can rescind the contract.

■ 5. Duress

A contract which is induced by a wrongful act, causing the other party to make decisions not of their own free will, is voidable by the aggrieved party. A person's free will is judged under a subjective standard, i.e., was the will of the particular person overcome, not whether a reasonable person's will would have been overcome. Taking advantage of another's economic needs is not normally considered duress.

West's Key No. Digests, Contracts ☞ 95. (95k95)

■ 6. Undue Influence

The term "undue influence" refers to a contract induced by a person in a fiduciary or psychological relationship with a party, when the controlling person occupies a position of trust and confidence. Such a contract is voidable by the subservient party.

CASEBOOK EXAMPLE: *Methodist Mission Home v. N.A.B.*, 451 S.W.2d 539 (Tex. Civ. App. 1970)
A single and pregnant woman sought refuge in a maternity home. She was convinced by the home to give up her child for adoption right after birth. When she sued to regain custody, the court ruled that the special relationship of the home, and its improper persuasion, constituted undue influence, and justified annulment of the adoption.

West's Key No. Digests, Contracts ☞ 96. (95k96)

III. Public Policy Defenses

A. ILLEGALITY

West's Key No. Digests, Contracts ☞ 101-142. (95I(F))

■ 1. Void or Voidable

An illegal contract is *void* if the subject matter of the contract is illegal. The contract does not legally exist. A contract is *voidable* if the *purpose* of the contract is illegal. It can be revoked, but only if actions are taken.

If an initially legal contract is rendered illegal by a new statute, the performances are discharged under the doctrine of impossibility. No party to an illegal contract may enforce it, even if one party's consideration, promise, or performance is legal.

■ 2. Illegal Subject

If the very subject of the contract is illegal, such as contracts for gambling, usurious interest, bribery, or to induce breach of fiduciary obligations, the contract is void from the beginning.

■ 3. Illegal Purpose

If a contract itself is legal, such as renting a car to another, but the purpose of the contract is illegal, such as using the rental car to rob a bank, the contract is voidable by the innocent party.

B. UNCONSCIONABILITY

An unconscionable contract, or an unconscionable clause in a contract, is one that is grossly unfair to one of the parties, usually because of stronger bargaining powers of the other party. It is one only a coerced or deluded person would make, and which no honest minded person would accept, because the terms are excessively extreme and one-sided.

West's Key No. Digests, Contracts ⚮ 1. (95k1)

■ 1. Common Law and UCC

If a contract is completely or partially unconscionable at the time it was made, it is unenforceable as a whole or in part. This defense applies both to common law contracts and those under the UCC (UCC § 2-302).

■ 2. Question for Court

Unconscionability is a mixed question of law and fact decided not by a jury, but by a court. The court will consider the setting, the purpose, and effect of the contract in determining whether it is unconscionable. The court can reform or void the contract, or remove (*sever*) an offending clause.

■ 3. Procedural Test

Unconscionability can be found because of the circumstances existing at the time the contract was formed. If one side had too unfair an advantage because of the superior bargaining position of the other party, a court may choose not to enforce it, because the disadvantaged party had no meaningful choice.

■ **4. Substantive Test**

Unconscionability can exist because of the terms of the contract. If terms are unreasonably favorable to one party, a court may choose not to enforce them.

> **CASEBOOK EXAMPLE:** *Williams v. Walker-Thomas*, 350 F.2d 445 (D.C. Cir. 1965) Ms. Williams purchased numerous household appliances from a store over a period of four years. The credit purchases were cross-collateralized. This gave the store the right to repossess everything, when even one item was not paid for on time. This included repossessing items fully paid for years earlier. The court ruled that the cross-collateralization clause was unconscionable.

IV. Enforcement Defense

A. PRINCIPLE OF STATUTE OF FRAUDS

The Statute of Frauds is a special statute requiring that some tangible evidence, such as a writing or performance, is needed to make certain contracts enforceable.

Spoken words—oral evidence—are insufficient. The Statute does not apply to all contracts, just those that are very valuable or those that might be easily misconstrued. The contracts covered include those for the sale of more than $500 of goods; contracts for the sale of land; contracts which cannot be performed within a year; contracts to guarantee the debt of another; and contracts made in anticipation of, i.e., consideration of, marriage.

West's Key No. Digests, Frauds, Statute of ☞ 121. (185k121)

B. TANGIBLE EVIDENCE

The tangible evidence that is required to prove that a contract covered by the Statute of Frauds was made can take several forms.

West's Key No. Digests, Frauds, Statute of ☞ 97-118. (185VIII)

■ **1. Writing**

The Statute is satisfied by a writing that states, with reasonable certainty, the parties, the subject matter, the terms and conditions, and is signed by the party against whom the contract is enforced.

> **CASEBOOK EXAMPLE:** *Crabtree v. Elizabeth Arden,* 110 N.E.2d 551 (N.Y. 1953)
> An employee of the Arden Company sued for breach of his employment contract, claiming that he did not receive the proper salary. The contract had been for two years. There were signed payroll cards, an unsigned management memo about the contract, but no overall written contract. The court ruled that the cards, viewed together with the memo, were sufficient to satisfy the need for tangible evidence.

■ 2. Performance

The Statute can be satisfied by full or part performance. However, a contract is enforceable only to the extent of the performance rendered.

> **CASEBOOK EXAMPLE:** *Cohn v. Fischer,* 287 A.2d 222 (N.J. Super. Ct. 1972)
> The buyer of a boat gave the seller a check for 50 percent as a down payment, but later stopped payment and refused to consummate the purchase. There was no other written contract. The seller sued. The court ruled that the check constituted part performance and satisfied the Statute of Frauds, making the contract enforceable.

■ 3. Promissory Estoppel

When detrimental reliance on the existence of a contract is both reasonable and foreseeable, and if manifest injustice would otherwise result, a contract can be enforced even though it does not otherwise meet the requirements of the Statute. *Detrimental reliance* occurs when a party relied on the promise of another in a reasonable way, and in a way in which they would be harmed if the promise were not fulfilled.

> **CASEBOOK EXAMPLE:** *Alaska Airlines v. Stephenson,* 217 F.2d 295 (9th Cir. 1954)
> A pilot quit his job, moved from California to Alaska, and went to work for Alaska Airlines, based on an oral agreement. The pilot and the airlines planned to work out a long-term written agreement later. When the pilot was laid off and sued for violation of the oral agreement, the court ruled that the employee's right to recover was not barred by the Statute of Frauds.

C. TYPES OF CONTRACTS COVERED

■ 1. Real Estate

The Statute applies to any promise to purchase, sell, mortgage, or transfer any interest in real property, including estates, leases, and easements. Licenses, leases, and easements for one year or less are excluded. A change of possession, partial or full payment, or completed improvements satisfy the Statute.

West's Key No. Digests, Frauds, Statute of ☞ 55-80. (185VI)

a. Crops, Timber, and Minerals

The sale of crops is not an interest in land and need not be in writing. Under the UCC, a timber sale contract must be in writing only if title to the timber passes before the trees are cut. The sale of minerals (or gas and oil) must be in writing only if the buyer removes them from the property.

b. Agent's Authority

Usually a writing signed by the buyer's agent is enforceable against the buyer, even though the agent's authority is orally granted. A few states follow the *equal dignity rule*: If an agent's act must be in writing, the agency agreement must also be.

■ 2. Sale of $500 in Goods

A contract, as drafted or modified, for the sale of goods for $500 or more is not enforceable unless in writing and signed by the party sought to be charged (UCC § 2-201). The writing must also include an accurate statement of the quantity of the goods. Other tangible evidence may be used to prove the existence of a contract in certain cases.

West's Key No. Digests, Frauds, Statute of ☞ 81-86. (185VII(A))

a. Merchant's Confirming Memo

In a contract between merchants, if one receives a signed, written confirmation within a reasonable time, the Statute is satisfied, if the receiving merchant had reason to know of the memo's contents and does not object within ten days.

b. Specially Manufactured Goods

If goods are specially manufactured for the buyer, are not suitable for sale to others, are in the ordinary course of the seller's business, and the seller has begun or committed to manufacturing them, the contract need not be in writing.

c. Judicial Admission

A writing is not required if the party against whom enforcement is sought admits, in a judicial context, that a contract was formed.

■ 3. Leases for $1,000

A contract for the lease of goods for $1,000 or more is not enforceable unless it is written and signed by the party against whom enforcement is sought (UCC § 2A-201).

West's Key No. Digests, Frauds, Statute of ☞ 57. (185k57)

■ 4. Not Performable in a Year

If a contract, by its own terms, cannot be fully performed within one year from formation of the contract, the Statute applies.

If there is any way that the contract *could* have been completely performed within a year, the Statute will not apply, even if the performance, in fact, lasts longer than a year. For example, if a company orally offers lifetime employment to a potential employee who accepts, the Statute does not apply because the employee *could* have died right after beginning work, fully performing the contract.

If contract performance will last longer than a year, but the parties reserve the right to terminate sooner, the right to terminate is not the same as a complete performance and the Statute still applies.

> **CASEBOOK EXAMPLE:** *Strasser v. Prudential Securities, Inc.*, 630 N.Y.S.2d 80 (N.Y. App. Div. 1995)
> The plaintiff in a lawsuit claimed that the defendant had an oral contract to provide financial assistance indefinitely. The plaintiff had the ability to terminate the agreement upon a breach by the defendant. The court ruled that the contract was covered by the Statute as not being performable within one year, because a breach and termination cannot be equated with performance.

West's Key No. Digests, Frauds, Statute of ☞ 43-54.5. (185V)

■ 5. Suretyship

A promise made to pay the debt of another is covered by the Statute. The surety's promise must be collateral or secondary. If the main purpose of the guarantee is to further the promisor's own interests, the Statute does not apply.

> **EXAMPLES:** (1) Junior wants to buy a new van, to be a courier for the family business. The dealer won't sell the van to Junior unless his dad guarantees payment. Dad does, because he needs a courier. Because dad's main purpose is to advance his own business interests, the Statute does not apply.
>   (2) Junior wants to buy a new van, to enjoy the summer following graduation. The dealer won't sell the van to Junior unless his dad guarantees payment. Dad does, because he feels that's what fathers do. Because Dad's main purpose is not to advance his own interests, the Statute applies.

West's Key No. Digests, Frauds, Statute of ☞ 13-36. (185III)

■ 6. In Consideration of Marriage

Contracts made in consideration of marriage, other than the parties' mutual promise to marry, must be in writing. This includes promises made by the couple, as well as other interested parties.

> **EXAMPLE:** A mother is convinced that her daughter should marry a certain suitor. To encourage the daughter, mother promises to hire the bride for the family business if she marries the suitor. The promise must be in writing.

West's Key No. Digests, Frauds, Statute of ☞ 1-6. (185I)

PART FIVE: CONDITIONS

OVERVIEW:
When a contract has been formed, the parties have promised to do something. Frequently, those promises are qualified or made contingent upon the occurrence of some other circumstances which might or might not occur. A qualifying circumstance is called a *condition*. For example, if someone contracts to buy a sports car for $400 as soon as they receive their next paycheck, one **condition precedent** is that the paycheck arrive. This means a condition which *precedes* the obligation. Until the paycheck arrives, the obligation to sell the car does not arise. Thus, contracting parties' promises to perform may have no immediate consequences due to conditions in the contract.

A promise for which there is no condition precedent must automatically be performed. For example, if someone contracts to simply buy a sports car for $400, the obligation to buy is immediate.

Conditions must be either satisfied or excused before the duty to perform arises. A condition is excused when the condition need no longer occur before performance of the duty becomes due. The non-occurrence of a condition may be excused on a variety of grounds, such as a subsequent promise. These are discussed below.

On the other hand, the conditions themselves create no rights or duties. They are simply *promise modifiers*. Whether a provision is an obligation or a condition can be very important.

EXAMPLE: An insurer and a home owner enter into a contract that provides: "Insurer will reimburse the owner for any losses resulting from fire. The owner will not store any flammable materials on his property." The home burns to the ground.

It turns out that the owner had stored gasoline in his garage, though the gasoline did not contribute to the fire. If the flammable materials provision is interpreted as a promise, the owner breached the contract, but the insurer can only recover damages for the breach. The insurer must still reimburse the owner for the fire damage. However, if the flammable material provision is viewed as a *condition precedent,* its violation means that the insurer's obligation never came due, and the owner would get no reimbursement.

I. Distinguishing Conditions from Promises

Courts use the standard rules of contract interpretation in deciding whether a contract provision is a promise or a condition. Included are the following.

West's Key No. Digests, Contracts ☞ 218. (95k218)

A. PARTIES' INTENT

The intent of the parties is given priority. The parties are free to designate a term as a condition if they so wish (R2d § 226(a)).

B. WORDING

No particular form of words is necessary, although the words "if," "on the condition that," or "provided that," when qualifying a promise, often indicate a condition. For example, in the contract offer "I will sell you my old sports car *provided* that I get the job I just applied for," getting the job is a condition precedent for the promise to sell the sports car (R2d § 226).

C. BILATERAL CONTRACTS

Courts disfavor interpretations that completely discharge a duty. Thus, in an ambiguous bilateral contract, a court will likely find that a provision creates a promise rather than a condition, especially if the condition is within the obligee's control (R2d § 227). The law abhors a complete forfeiture of rights by either party.

> **EXAMPLE:** An insurer and a homeowner made a contract that provided: "Insurer will reimburse the owner for any losses resulting from fire. The owner will not store any flammable materials on his property." The home burned to the ground. It turns out that the owner had stored gasoline in his garage, though that did not contribute to the fire. If there is litigation, a court will conclude that the flammable materials provision was a promise, not a condition precedent. Otherwise, the insurance company will have no duty to perform, i.e., pay for the fire damage.

D. UNILATERAL CONTRACTS

If a unilateral contract is proposed, a court will usually find that an ambiguous provision is a condition rather than a promise, since the offeree never makes a promise to perform in a unilateral contract.

> **EXAMPLE:** A homeowner offered to pay a landscaper $400 to mow his lawn before 5 P.M. on Friday, when the homeowner was having a party. The landscaper did the job on Saturday morning. If the 5 P.M. term was a promise, then the homeowner would still have to pay, although the landscaper would be in breach of contract and liable for minimal, i.e., nominal, damages. If the 5 P.M. term was a condition precedent, then there is no contract and the homeowner's duty does not arise.

E. SATISFACTION REQUIRED

In cases involving personal taste, a contract is often dependent on, i.e., conditioned on, satisfaction guaranteed. This might appear to allow a complete escape from the contract by the one who must be satisfied after they have received the benefits under the contract.

To avoid an unjust result, contract law solves this issue by applying a good faith subjective test when one party's duty is conditioned upon subjective satisfaction, such as in art or personal taste. This means in practice that one party must be satisfied, but it must be reasonable and honest satisfaction, not just an excuse to get out of a contract because of buyer's remorse (R2d § 228).

If a contract provides that the promisor's performance (i.e., payment) is conditioned not upon the promisor's approval, but rather on that of a third party (e.g., an architect or engineer), the promisor need not perform if the third party is not satisfied under the same good faith subjective standard as for a contracting party directly.

> **EXAMPLES:** (1) A person contracted with a painter to paint his portrait for $1,000, and told the painter beforehand that he was very picky, and must be satisfied or he would not pay. The finished portrait was unrecognizable and the subject would not pay. The subject was not in breach of the contract and need not pay the painter. The subject's expression of dissatisfaction was made in good faith.
>
> (2) A homeowner offers to pay a landscaper $400 to mow his lawn, and tells the landscaper beforehand that he is very picky, and must be satisfied. The landscaper does a good job and meets the standard of quality for the profession. However the homeowner would not pay, because he had just watched the Master's golf tournament on TV and wants his lawn to look like the putting greens at Augusta. The homeowner is in breach and is liable to the landscaper for damages. The homeowner's sense of satisfaction is unreasonable and made in bad faith.

II. Types of Conditions

A. CONDITIONS PRECEDENT

These are events, other than a lapse of time, that must occur *before* a duty to perform arises. In any dispute, a plaintiff would have the burden of proving the existence and satisfaction of conditions precedent.

> **EXAMPLE:** A buyer contracted to buy a new car. The contract was contingent upon the buyer obtaining financing within 30 days. The financing was a *condition precedent* to the promise to buy. If the financing is obtained, the buyer must go through with the purchase.

West's Key No. Digests, Contracts ☞ 221. (95k221)

B. CONCURRENT CONDITIONS

Concurrent conditions exist if the parties are to exchange performances at the same time. Neither party must perform unless the other has offered (*tendered*) performance. If one party fails to tender performance, the other party is excused from doing so. In any dispute, a plaintiff would have the burden of proving the existence and satisfaction of concurrent conditions.

> **EXAMPLE:** A student contracted with a friend to sell his sports car for $400. The student's readiness to part with the car is a concurrent condition, along with the friend's readiness to part with $400. If only one tenders performance, the other is in breach. If one does not tender performance, the other is not required to perform.

West's Key No. Digests, Contracts ☞ 225. (95k225)

C. CONDITIONS SUBSEQUENT

These are events that operate to discharge a duty to perform *after* the duty has arisen. In any dispute, the party attempting to avoid the contract duty would have the burden of proving that the *condition subsequent* justified forfeiture of the duty to perform.

> **EXAMPLE:** A student has an insurance policy guarding against theft. The policy requires that notice of any theft must be given within ten days for the loss to be covered. If a thief steals the student's computer, unless the condition subsequent requiring notice is satisfied or excused, the insurance company's duty to pay will be discharged. The company would have the burden of proving the lack of notice and the existence of the condition.

West's Key No. Digests, Contracts ☞ 226. (95k226)

D. EXPRESS CONDITIONS

If the parties expressly agree that an event must occur, or not occur, before a duty to perform arises, the condition is an express condition. It will usually be preceded with words such as "on the condition that," "only if," or "provided that." A party must comply strictly with an express provision before the other party's duty arises.

West's Key No. Digests, Contracts ☞ 219. (95k219)

E. CONSTRUCTIVE CONDITIONS

A constructive condition is a condition that is implied as a matter of law. If the occurrence of an event is within the control of one of the parties, there is always an implied condition—a promise to use reasonable, good faith efforts to cause the condition to occur. For example, if the contract is conditioned upon the purchaser obtaining financing, the purchaser must make a good faith effort to obtain financing. If parties fail to state or make clear the order in which their respective promises are to be performed, a court will supply the order based on the doctrine of constructive condition, implied by law.

West's Key No. Digests, Contracts ☞ 220. (95k220)

■ 1. If One Performance Precedes Another
The first party's performance is a condition to the second party's.

■ 2. If One Performance Takes Longer
The longer performance by one party is a condition to the shorter performance by the other party.

■ 3. If Both Performances Are Simultaneous
Both performances then are conditioned upon each other. Thus, if under the terms of the contract, A is to purchase B's car for $400, A need not pay the $400 until B tenders the car and B need not transfer the car until A tenders the $400.

III. Excusing Conditions

Even if a condition which modifies some contract promise has not yet occurred, a party's duty to perform arises if the condition is *excused*. The condition then is removed (*severed*) from the contract. The duty which was previously conditioned or qualified then becomes due.

Conditions may be excused by voluntary methods, such as waiver or estoppel. Conditions may also be excused by punitive principles, such as hindrance or *anticipatory repudiation*.

A. VOLUNTARY EXCUSES

West's Key No. Digests, Contracts ☞ 227. (95k227)

■ 1. Waiver
Waiver is the express renunciation of a known right. If a party makes it clear by words or conduct that a condition need not occur before performing, the condition is waived and it disappears.

◼ 2. Estoppel

If a party suggested an intention to waive a condition; or if a party suggested indifference to a condition, by words or conduct; and if the other party changed position in reasonable reliance on the suggested waiver of the condition; then the first party may be estopped from requiring occurrence of the condition before performance.

> **EXAMPLES:** (1) A buyer accepts a shipment of goods from a seller, even though it did not match the original specifications—it was *nonconforming.* The seller could have later sold the goods to another dealer, but relied upon the buyer's acceptance. The buyer may not revoke his acceptance later.
>
> (2) A buyer accepts a shipment of goods from a seller, even though it did not match the original specifications; it was *nonconforming.* The buyer's acceptance was made under the belief that the nonconformity would be later cured. If the nonconformity was not cured, the buyer may then revoke his acceptance (UCC § 2-607).

B. PUNITIVE EXCUSES

West's Key No. Digests, Contracts ☞ 278(1). (95k278(1))

◼ 1. Prevention or Hindrance

If one party's performance is a condition precedent to the second party's performance and the second party engages in wrongful conduct that prevents the first party from performing, the condition is excused and the second party is required to perform. Wrongful conduct may include passive noncooperation as well as an overt act.

> **EXAMPLE:** A real estate sales contract is conditioned on the buyer obtaining financing. There is an implied promise that the buyer will make a good faith effort to obtain it. If the buyer intentionally avoids obtaining financing, thus making it impossible for the seller to perform, the buyer will not be allowed to refuse the financing condition. He must go through with the purchase anyway.

◼ 2. Anticipatory Repudiation

Anticipatory repudiation is an assertion or unequivocal forecast by a party to a contract that she will not perform a future obligation required by the contract when it is due. This occurs when a party to an incomplete (*executory*) contract manifests a definite and unequivocal intent not to render the performance due by the contract when the time arrives.

a. Effect

A repudiated duty becomes immediately due, and a present breach of contract occurs. This excuses nonperformance by the other party. In such a case the other party may treat the contract as ended. A repudiation may be retracted until a lawsuit or detrimental reliance occurs.

b. Forms of Repudiation

A party can repudiate a contract by an overt declaration or expression of intent, or through conduct, when the party manifests a *prospective inability to perform* when required.

> **EXAMPLES:** (1) A supplier of construction materials contracted to sell lumber to a home builder for the next several years. The supplier's lumber costs rose precipitously, and it notified the builder that in the future, it would not supply lumber at the original price. This was an *overt declaration of anticipatory repudiation*. The builder need not wait until the next order; it could immediately declare the supplier in breach and sue for damages.
>
> (2) A supplier of construction materials contracted to sell lumber to a home builder for a current project. But before actually supplying the lumber, the supplier sold his entire stock to another builder, and decided to go on an extended cruise. This constituted anticipatory repudiation through conduct, by showing a *prospective inability to perform*. The builder need not wait until the next order; she could immediately declare the supplier in breach and sue for damages.

c. Ambiguity

The repudiating statement or conduct must be unambiguous. Statements of doubt or ambiguous conduct regarding a party's inability or unwillingness to perform are insufficient. However, if a party has made an ambiguous statement about whether performance will occur, the other party may demand *adequate assurances of performance* in writing. Failure to give adequate assurances within a reasonable time—not longer than 30 days under the UCC—will be a repudiation.

d. Common Law Responses

A party may respond to an anticipatory repudiation in several ways under a common law contract:

1. Bring suit immediately for total breach of contract.
2. Ignore the repudiation and insist on performance.
3. Suspend performance and sue after actual failure to perform.
4. Simply treat the obligee's own duties as being discharged.

e. UCC Responses

A party may respond to an anticipatory repudiation in several ways under a UCC contract, if the loss of performance substantially impairs the value of the contract (UCC § 2-610):

1. Wait, but only for a commercially reasonable time.
2. Resort to any remedy, even after first declaring forbearance.
3. Suspend performance of the contract.

IV. Satisfying Conditions

Finally, conditions that are not excused must be satisfied in order to trigger the applicable party's duty to perform. Depending upon the type of condition, they may be satisfied by complete (*perfect*) satisfaction, *substantial* satisfaction, or through *division*.

West's Key No. Digests, Contracts ⟷ 278(1). (95k278(1))

A. PERFECT SATISFACTION

If the parties have expressly stated a condition in the contract, the condition must be completely satisfied to cause the duties to be performable. The condition must occur exactly as the parties contemplated.

> **EXAMPLE:** A homeowner contracted with a landscaper to have his lawn mowed for $400. The homeowner tells the landscaper that the grass must be no longer than one-half inch tall for an upcoming game of miniature golf or the homeowner will not pay. The landscaper does the job, but the cut grass is two inches tall. The landscaper violated an express condition, so the homeowner need not pay.

Also, in a single delivery of goods under the UCC, the *Perfect Tender Rule* requires the seller to deliver conforming goods, at the agreed time, with the correct method of tender. Failure in the tender of delivery relieves the buyer of performance, **except that the seller must be given a commercially reasonable opportunity to cure any defects.**

B. SUBSTANTIAL SATISFACTION

Frequently, contract conditions aren't spelled out in great detail. When conditions are only implied, or expressed vaguely, *substantial compliance* with them is sufficient. Substantial compliance means compliance with all the essential requirements of a condition, when any deviations are trifling, and the benefit of the contract is not materially diminished.

Substantial compliance is the legal equivalent of full performance or compliance.

> **EXAMPLE:** A homeowner contracted with a landscaper to have his lawn mowed for $400. There is no further discussion between them. The landscaper does the job and meets the standard of quality for the profession. The job is not perfect. However, the landscaper has substantially complied and the homeowner must pay the landscaper.

C. SATISFACTION BY DIVISION

Some contracts are divisible into independent acts, each of which confers a separate benefit, and for which a separate, reciprocal duty is owed. For purposes of excusing constructive conditions, these divisible contracts are treated as a series of separate contracts. This is done in order to avoid forfeiture of all the contracts, which would be too severe a result.

> **EXAMPLE:** A student contracts with a classmate to make him dinner each Friday during the winter for $20 per meal. Since the contract is divisible into separate units, making each meal is considered to be a constructive condition to each equivalent payment. Payment is due after each meal, not in the spring. The completion of all the meals is not necessary as a condition precedent to the student's duty to pay.

PART SIX: DISCHARGE AND PERFORMANCE

OVERVIEW:

Once a contract has been formed, properly interpreted, and all conditions have been excused or satisfied, the parties stand on the threshold of fulfilling the purpose of the contract. This they must then do, unless some event or change in circumstances arises after formation of the contract and *discharges* the duty to perform. Thus, *discharge* or *performance* of duties are the choices confronting the contracting parties at this point in the unfolding of a contract.

There are four legal theories which discharge otherwise valid contractual duties: *Impossibility, impracticability, frustration of purpose,* and *conditions subsequent.* These theories are used by the law to intervene and discharge contractual duties when injustice would otherwise result.

There are also four types of new agreements that have the same effect: *Modification, rescission, accord and satisfaction,* and *novation.* These are really new contracts, with the same fundamental requirements of any contract, requiring offer, acceptance, and consideration.

I. Legal Theories of Discharge

A. IMPOSSIBILITY

If events occur that make it impossible for any reasonable person to perform a contract, those duties may be discharged.

The doctrine only applies to unforeseeable events that occur after formation of the contract, when the parties did not allocate or assume the risk for the events (*a supervening impossibility*). The impossibility must be objective. The test is: "The thing cannot be done," not "I cannot do it" (R2d § 261, Comment e).

West's Key No. Digests, Contracts ☞ 303(1); Sales ☞ 171. (95k303(1), 343k171)

■ 1. Destruction of Subject Matter

The subject matter of a contract is the contract's reason for being—its *raison d'être*. When the subject matter of a contract or the means by which it would be performed is destroyed through no fault of the promisor, his contractual duties are discharged. The subject matter must be referred to in the contract or the parties must have understood it was included.

■ **CASEBOOK EXAMPLE:** *Taylor v. Caldwell*, 122 Eng. Rep. 309 (K.B. 1863)
A singer contracted to perform in a certain auditorium, which burned down before the concert. The auditorium was ruled the basis of the performance, so the contract was discharged.

NOTE—*Distinctive Rule for Real Property:* In contracts for real property, most courts apply the doctrine of *equitable conversion,* and unless the contract otherwise provides, allocate the risk of loss to the prospective purchaser, though legal title has not yet been transferred. The doctrine provides that, once parties have entered into a binding and enforceable land sale contract, the purchaser's interest is said to be real property and seller's retained interest is characterized as personal property. The rights of the parties are evaluated as if the conveyance had been made. Many states, however, have by statute changed the common law rule and leave the risk with the seller unless the contract otherwise provides.

■ 2. UCC Casualty Rules

In contracts for the sale of goods, if the contract is impossible to perform because of destruction of the subject matter, the risk of loss is allocated by the UCC, unless otherwise stated in the contract (UCC § 2-501).

A seller retains responsibility for goods until the risk of loss passes to the buyer. Thus, a contract for identified goods is voided if the goods are totally destroyed through no fault of either party, before the risk of loss passes to the buyer (UCC § 2-613(a)). The rules regulating when the risk of loss passes from the seller to the buyer are stated below.

a. The Contract Controls

Under the UCC, the risk of loss is initially contractual rather than dependent upon who has title to the goods, as it is at common law. The parties may allocate risk as they wish. The risk is the owner-seller's until an agreement or event occurs to shift the risk to the buyer (UCC § 2-509). If there is no explicit allocation of risk, then other UCC principles govern.

b. No Destination Specified

If a contract requires the seller to ship goods by common carrier and does not require a particular destination, the risk of loss passes to the buyer when the seller has made a reasonable contract for delivery and delivered the goods to the carrier (UCC § 2-509).

c. Destination Specified

If a contract requires the seller to deliver the goods at a particular destination (f.o.b.), the risk of loss only passes to the buyer when the goods are tendered to the buyer at that destination.

d. Direct Dealing

When merchants are dealing directly, the risk of loss is assumed by the buyer when the goods are physically delivered. For nonmerchants, the risk of loss is assumed by the buyer when the goods are offered, i.e., at tender of delivery (UCC § 2-509(c)).

e. Bailments

If goods are to be picked up by the buyer from a bailee, such as a warehouser, the risk of loss passes to the buyer upon receipt of title, or upon the bailee's acknowledgment of the buyer's right to possession.

f. Seller's Breach

A seller who breaches retains the risk of loss, if the tender or delivery is so defective as to give the buyer a right to reject the goods. The risk of loss will then pass to the buyer only if the seller cures the breach or the buyer accepts the goods.

EXAMPLE: A toymaker contracted to buy $1,000 worth of model train parts. The manufacturer mistakenly sent $1,000 of toy truck parts to his usual shipper. But the toy

> truck parts were stolen in route. The buyer would have been liable if the shipment were conforming, but since the tender was defective, the loss was retained by the seller.

g. Buyer's Breach

A buyer who breaches a contract before the risk of loss has passed to him, then bears the risk of loss, for a commercially reasonable time, if the goods are identified and conforming. Since the buyer *should* have accepted the goods, he becomes liable for their destruction until an alternate sale can be arranged.

■ 3. Destruction of Agreed or Sole Source

If contracting parties specify a certain source for the subject matter of the contract, or in fact there is only one, destruction of that source renders performance impossible (UCC § 2-615(a)).

> **EXAMPLE:** A woodworker contracted to panel the office of a customer with rare Brazilian rosewood. Before work could begin, civil war broke out in Brazil and the few remaining stands of rosewood were destroyed. The woodworker's duty under the contract was excused by the doctrine of impossibility.

■ 4. Death or Incapacity of Performer

If a contract specifically calls for a particular performer, such as in a personal services contract, and the performer dies or becomes incapacitated, the parties are discharged from performing the contract.

West's Key No. Digests, Contracts ⧉ 311. (95k311)

■ 5. Supervening Illegality

If a contract is legal at the time it is formed, but the parties' performances are later rendered illegal by a change in a statute, the contract duties are accordingly discharged.

> **EXAMPLE:** A well digger contracts to dig a well for an urban house. Before beginning, the city passes an ordinance preventing the digging of wells. The supervening illegality discharges the digger's duties under the contract.

■ 6. Temporary Impossibility

If performance is only temporarily impossible, that duty is not discharged, but merely suspended until the impossibility ends.

B. IMPRACTICABILITY

Contract duties can be discharged by an unforeseen occurrence that the parties assumed would not occur, if it creates an unanticipated and unreasonable difficulty. The reverse is equally true: Contract duties can be discharged by an unforeseen non-occurrence that the parties assumed would occur, if it creates an unanticipated and unreasonable difficulty. Under the UCC, the duties of a seller will be discharged if performance has been made impracticable, judged from a commercial perspective (UCC § 2-615).

> **CASEBOOK EXAMPLE:** *Mineral Park v. Howard,* **172 Cal. 289 (1916)**
> A bridge builder contracted with a quarry for a supply of gravel. The contract was at a fixed price, for all the gravel needed for a bridge project—known as a requirements contract. Subsequently, the quarry unexpectedly flooded, making the gravel ten times as expensive to recover. The builder was excused from further performance.

West's Key No. Digests, Contracts ☞ 303. (95k303)

C. FRUSTRATION OF PURPOSE

When a supervening event occurs that totally or substantially frustrates the principal purpose for a contract, performance will be discharged. The purpose must be a mutual assumption; the event must be unanticipated; it must occur through no fault of the frustrated party. Under the UCC, frustration of purpose by seller is judged even more strictly, analogous to the principles of impossibility, discussed above. The seller must show that the sale cannot be made by anyone, not merely that the seller cannot make it.

> **CASEBOOK EXAMPLE:** *2814 Food Corp. v. Hub Bar Building Corp.,* **297 N.Y.S.2d 762 (Sup. Ct. 1969)**
> A tenant contracted to lease premises for ten years for a supermarket. While the tenant was making improvements and installing equipment, and before the supermarket opened, the city gave notice that it would take over the property for a school. The tenant sued to rescind the lease. The court ruled that since the tenant never used the premises, there was frustration of purpose, and the tenant was entitled to recover the security deposit and rent paid.

West's Key No. Digests, Contracts ☞ 303. (95k303)

D. CONDITIONS SUBSEQUENT

If the parties have expressly stated a condition subsequent in their contract, failure to excuse or satisfy the condition will discharge the duties under the contract.

> **EXAMPLE:** A student has an insurance policy guarding against theft. The policy requires that notice of any theft must be given within ten days for the loss to be covered. If a thief steals the student's computer, unless the condition subsequent requiring notice is satisfied by the student or excused by the insurer, the insurance company's duty to pay will be discharged.

II. Discharge by New Agreement

A. MODIFICATION

West's Key No. Digests, Contracts ⟷ 236-248. (95III)

■ 1. Definition
Modification occurs when the parties to an unfulfilled (executory) contract modify it, and change a duty of performance already due from one or more parties.

■ 2. Effect
Substituting a new promise for one already due under the contract would appear to warrant application of the preexisting duty rule, discussed above, and would appear to make the modifications invalid. However, under both the common law and the UCC, the parties to an existing contract can make a new agreement that discharges the original duties and imposes new ones.

■ 3. Common Law Contracts
For contracts covered by the common law, a new agreement must be a complete, enforceable contract to be effective, with offer, acceptance, and consideration. If a party is under a preexisting duty to perform the duties called for by the modified contract, that party must give consideration for the release of the preexisting duty or the modification contract is invalid. The modification (second) contract must be in writing if the original contract was so required. The modification discharges those original terms that are covered by the modification and imposes new obligations. If there are remaining terms outside the scope of a new agreement, they still must be performed.

■ 4. UCC Contracts
The rule is different for contracts covered by the UCC. If the parties, in good faith, agree to modify a contract for the sale or lease of goods, no additional consideration is needed, even if a party was under a preexist-

ing duty under the original contract to do the same thing. In these cases, the UCC basically has abolished the preexisting duty rule. The modification must still be in writing if the original contract had to be (UCC §§ 2-209 and 2A-208).

EXAMPLES: (1) A toymaker contracted to have his showroom painted within a month for $300. The painter later said that he could not meet the schedule. The painter proposed a new agreement, with the painting to be done for $400. The toymaker agreed and the painting was completed. Under the common law, the new agreement was invalid since the painter provided no consideration. The painter could not collect the extra $100.

(2) A toymaker contracted to buy $400 worth of model trains to be delivered within a month. The manufacturer was unable to meet the production schedule, and proposed a new agreement, with the trains to be delivered a month later for the same price. The toymaker agreed. Under the UCC, the new agreement is valid, even though there was no new consideration for the toymaker. The original duties were discharged.

B. RESCISSION

The parties may agree to rescind, cancel, or release their contractual duties under the original contract. If the rescission is enforceable, the original duties are discharged. Both parties giving up their rights under the contract is adequate consideration to make the rescission binding.

West's Key No. Digests, Contracts ☜ 249-274. (95IV)

C. ACCORD AND SATISFACTION

Accord and satisfaction is a procedure for resolving contract disputes through compromise. One party offers a compromise to fulfill (*discharge*) an existing debt or duty and the other party accepts. The new, compromise agreement is called the *accord*. The *satisfaction* is the actual performance of the new agreement, which discharges both the old and new obligations. An agreement to compromise a bona fide dispute over money owed provides good consideration for each party, which is normally required with this procedure.

EXAMPLES: (1) A creditor claimed that a debtor owed him $5,000. The debtor sincerely claimed that he owed only $3,500. The debtor offered to pay the creditor $3,500 to discharge the entire debt. The creditor agreed (that is the accord). The creditor accepted the debtor's payment of $3,500 (that is the satisfaction). Even if the creditor originally had a valid claim for $5,000, he will be precluded from recovering the other $1,500.

(2) A creditor claimed that a debtor owed him $5,000. The debtor did not dispute the validity of that debt. The debtor offered to pay the creditor $3,500 as

full payment of the debt. The creditor agreed and took the $3,500 payment. Because there was no genuine dispute over the validity of the debt, the creditor's later promise to accept $3,500 was not supported by consideration. The creditor was not precluded from recovering the other $1,500.

NOTE—*Divergent Rule for Checks:* If a debtor writes on the check to a creditor, "Payment In Full," and if there is a genuine dispute, cashing the check operates as an accord and satisfaction. Under the UCC, a creditor may reserve the right to collect further, while still accepting the check, by indorsing it "under protest," or "without prejudice" (UCC § 1-207).

West's Key No. Digests, Accord and Satisfaction ⬳ 23. (8k23)

D. NOVATION

A novation is an agreement substituting a new party and/or performance for the original ones in a contract. It discharges the original parties and/or performance. The novation must be a complete, valid contract in its own right.

West's Key No. Digests, Novation ⬳ 10. (278k10)

III. Performance

If there are no reasons for discharge, the party is obligated to fulfill the contract duties by complete performance, substantial performance, or the doctrine of divisibility.

A. COMPLETE PERFORMANCE

If the parties have expressly stated a specific duty in the contract, it must be completely performed to avoid a breach of contract. The performance must occur exactly as the parties contemplated. If the parties have stated certain standards or requirements in the contract, they must be met.

Also, in a single delivery of goods under the UCC, the perfect tender rule requires the seller to deliver conforming goods, at the agreed time, with the correct method of tender. Failure in the tender of delivery relieves the buyer of performance, except that the seller must be given a commercially reasonable opportunity, even after the time for performance, to cure any defects.

If a party is ready, willing, and able to perform and tenders performance at the time it is due, that party's duty is discharged.

West's Key No. Digests, Contracts ⬳ 280, 281. (95k280, 95k281)

B. SUBSTANTIAL PERFORMANCE

Substantial performance means performance with all the essential requirements of a contract, when any deviations are trifling, and when the benefit of the contract is not materially diminished.

Substantial performance is the legal equivalent of full performance. In the absence of exact standards expressed in the contract, substantial performance is sufficient to fulfill contractual duties. The substantial performance doctrine is the standard used for most contracts.

West's Key No. Digests, Contracts 293. (95k293)

C. DIVISIBILITY

Some contracts are divisible into independent acts, each of which confers a separate benefit, and for which a separate, reciprocal duty is owed. For purposes of evaluating performance, these divisible contracts are treated as a series of separate contracts, analyzed duty by duty (R2d § 240). A party who performs a unit of a divisible contract may recover the agreed-upon equivalent for that part performance.

With an installment contract under the UCC, a buyer may reject a nonconforming installment only if the nonconformity substantially impairs the value of that installment and cannot be cured by the seller.

PART SEVEN: REMEDIES FOR BREACH

OVERVIEW:
After all conditions have been satisfied or excused, unless there is a discharge of a contract duty, a party must finally perform that duty. Failure to do so excuses the other party's duty and creates a breach of contract. The law then provides remedies to the innocent party, primarily in the form of money (*damages*), but also in the form of equitable relief, used when money cannot cure the loss created by the breach of contract.

The guiding principle of contract damages is to re-create the expected contract benefit to the aggrieved party. Thus, damages are said to place the injured party in the position she would have occupied had the contract been performed.

When there is no enforceable contract, or if damages cannot be adequately calculated, and the aggrieved party has changed position for the worse due to the wrongdoer's words or conduct, the injured party is entitled to compensation for the losses incurred in reliance upon the other party. Finally, when the aggrieved party has conferred a benefit upon the wrongdoer, the former is entitled to the return of the benefit conferred.

Damages include the loss of expected contract benefits (*expectation damages*); *liquidated damages*, predicted beforehand as an element of the original contract; and *compensatory damages,* for losses suffered in relying upon the expected contract obligations that were breached.

Equitable relief includes *rescission and restitution*, cancellation of the contract and refund of any benefits conferred; *reformation*, used when a written contract is inaccurate and should be amended; and *specific performance,* available when the damages remedy at law (money) is inadequate, such as when dealing with a unique piece of art or property.

I. Money Damages

The award of money damages is the most common method of compensating an innocent party when they are harmed by a party's failure to perform. The purpose of the remedy is to place innocent parties in the position they would have been in, had the contract not been breached. However, the remedy must be rational, not extravagant.

CASEBOOK EXAMPLE: *Jacob and Youngs v. Kent,* 129 N.E. 889 (1921)
A building contract required Reading pipe for all the plumbing. The builder used some Cohoes pipe. The homeowner wanted the Cohoes pipe replaced and sued. There was no difference in quality between the two brands and no difference in the value of the house. The court refused to order the pipe replacement, and awarded only nominal damages, finding that the cost of repair was in excess of any actual damages and would result in economic waste.

A. EXPECTATION DAMAGES

Expectation damages are the primary means of compensating an innocent party for the benefit of the bargain which was lost by the breach. The damages must be certain, not speculative.

CASEBOOK EXAMPLE: *Hawkins v. McGee,* 84 N.H. 114 (1929)
A surgeon told a young patient that after an operation on his scarred hand, it would be "100 percent perfect." It turned out to be hairy because of the type of skin graft used. The patient sued, and the court calculated damages as the difference between the value of the expected perfect hand, compared with the value of the hairy hand.

West's Key No. Digests, Damages ☞ 21, 117-126. (115k21, 115VI(C))

B. LIQUIDATED DAMAGES

Liquidated damages are those agreed upon in the original contract in the event of a breach. **They must be reasonable, and not really punishment, i.e., a penalty for breach of contract in disguise. They are permitted only when the potential damages would be difficult to calculate. If the contract contains a valid liquidated damages clause, and there is a breach of contract, actual damages need not be proven. A liquidated damages clause does not prohibit other available remedies.**

West's Key No. Digests, Damages 74-86. (115IV)

C. COMPENSATORY DAMAGES

Damages frequently take the form of compensatory damages, also known as *reliance* or *consequential damages*.

These are damages not from the contract real bargain itself, but from reliance on the contract performance.

They must be reasonably foreseeable—either a natural or probable result of the breach, or within the contemplation of the contracting parties.

> **CASEBOOK EXAMPLE:** *Hadley v. Baxendale,* 156 Eng. Rep. 145 (1854)
> Hadley contracted with Baxendale, a common carrier, to deliver a broken mill shaft to a foundry for repair. Because Baxendale took too long, Hadley had to close down his mill. He sued for lost profits. Because the shut down of the mill was not a reasonably foreseeable result of Baxendale's breach, damages for lost profits were rejected.

West's Key No. Digests, Damages 21. (115k21)

D. MITIGATION OF DAMAGES

The innocent party must always minimize (*mitigate*) damages caused by a breach.

If an innocent party has an opportunity to mitigate but does not, damages will be lessened by the amount that could have been saved. The innocent party must not let usable resources go to waste; they must obtain replacement goods to keep damages down; and wronged employees and employers must seek alternate employment.

West's Key No. Digests, Damages 62(4). (115k62(4))

E. PUNITIVE DAMAGES

Punitive damages are not usually awarded for breach of contract. However, if the breach is malicious or intentionally harmful and therefore similar to a tort, courts occasionally allow these damages.

West's Key No. Digests, Damages ⟐ 89(2). (115k89(2))

F. SALE OF GOODS—THE UCC

■ 1. Seller's Damages

If a buyer breaches a contract, the seller has the following choice of remedies.

West's Key No. Digests, Sales ⟐ 384. (343k384)

a. Commercial Resale

If a buyer breaches a contract, the seller can recover the difference at the time of breach between the contract price and the commercially reasonable resale value of the subject matter of the contract. The seller must notify the buyer unless the goods are perishable.

b. Market Price

If a buyer breaches a contract, the seller can recover the difference at the time of breach between the contract price and the market price of the subject matter of the contract.

c. Lost Profits

If a buyer breaches a contract, even if the goods are sold elsewhere, the seller can recover the profits lost because of the reduced sales volume (UCC § 2-708).

> **EXAMPLE:** A high-volume discount store contracts to sell a computer to a customer, but the customer later refuses to complete the purchase. Even if the store sells the same computer for the same price to another person, the store can sue the customer for the profits lost from the unfinished sale.

■ 2. Buyer's Damages

If a seller breaches a contract, the buyer has the following choice of remedies.

West's Key No. Digests, Sales ⟐ 418. (343k418)

a. Cover

If a seller breaches a contract, the buyer can "cover," that is recover the difference between the contract price and the price that must be paid to purchase replacement property without unreasonable delay.

b. Market Price

If a seller breaches a contract, the buyer can recover the difference at the time of breach between the contract price and the market price of the subject matter of the contract.

G. QUASI CONTRACT

To avoid an undeserved windfall, when a benefit has been given, or a cost incurred, the law creates quasi contracts. To prevent unjust enrichment, these are created by law when there was no ordinary contract or one was voided.

The preferred recovery for a quasi contract is the value of the benefit conferred.

If the performer has not conferred any benefit, but has incurred costs in preparing to perform, in reliance upon a potential contract, the performer may recover the costs.

> **EXAMPLES:** (1) Barney asked Andy to construct a fountain for him. They wrote nothing down, did not discuss price, and no valid contract was formed. Andy began work, but then Barney changed his mind and told Andy to stop. Andy can recover the actual value of the partially constructed fountain, the benefit conferred upon Barney.
> (2) Barney asked Andy to construct a fountain for him. They wrote nothing down, did not discuss price, and no valid contract was formed. In preparation, Andy brought in a team of masons and purchased materials. But before Andy could begin, Barney changed his mind. Andy's workers and materials did not benefit Barney, but they were a cost incurred by Andy in preparing to perform, which he can recover.

West's Key No. Digests, Implied and Constructive Contracts ⟜ 110. (205Hk110)

II. Equitable Remedies

Equitable remedies are only available when the legal remedies are inadequate, when there has been no unreasonable delay (*laches*), the party asking for the remedy is innocent of misbehavior (*clean hands*), and there is no undue hardship imposed by the remedy.

A. RESCISSION

Rescission cancels all the obligations of a void or voidable contract, in a similar manner as the annulment of a marriage. Rescission often is used if there was incapacity or mistake during formation of a contract, or it was induced by fraud, duress, or undue influence.

B. RESTITUTION

Restitution attempts to return to an innocent party some benefit conferred upon a wrongdoer. When it would be unjust to retain the benefit, the wrongdoer is returned to the condition she was in before the contract.

C. REFORMATION

A written contract may be reformed when, due to fraud or mistake, the writing does not accurately describe the actual agreement of the parties. A classic example is the correction of typographical errors.

West's Key No. Digests, Reformation of Instruments ⬅ 1-29. (328I)

D. SPECIFIC PERFORMANCE

Specific performance requires a party to produce the same effect as if a contract had been completed, or refrain from acts inconsistent with the contract. It is a method of enforcing a unique performance that cannot be substituted for by money.

Specific performance will be ordered only if it is feasible and fair to do so. The innocent party must tender performance, and the court must have mutual jurisdiction. Courts will not grant a remedy when they have to supervise compliance.

■ 1. Real Estate
All real estate contracts dealing with land are unique and thus specifically enforceable.

West's Key No. Digests, Specific Performance ⬅ 63. (358k63)

■ 2. Sale of Goods
Goods may be unique and their sale specifically enforceable. Obvious cases are goods that are one of a kind, such as art or an heirloom.

West's Key No. Digests, Specific Performance ⬅ 67. (358k67)

■ 3. Personal Service Contracts
Contracts for personal service generally cannot be delegated, involving persons such as athletes and entertainers. Courts will not specifically order a service performed, but they will grant injunctions prohibiting the person from entering into competing arrangements.

West's Key No. Digests, Specific Performance ⬅ 73. (358k73)

E. UCC REMEDIES

■ **1. Sale of Special Goods**

A buyer can force the sale of special goods, even if not unique, when it would be unreasonably burdensome to obtain comparable goods (UCC § 2-716(1)).

West's Key No. Digests, Sales ⟿ 384(6). (343k384(6))

■ **2. Action for the Price**

A seller can bring an *action for the price* when a buyer who failed to pay has accepted goods; the risk of loss has passed to him; or unaccepted goods cannot be reasonably resold. This method is really a forced sale of the goods (UCC § 2-709).

West's Key No. Digests, Sales ⟿ 340-368. (343VII(E))

PART EIGHT: NONPARTY RIGHTS AND DUTIES

OVERVIEW:

People who are not parties to a contract normally have no rights or duties resulting from the contract. However, contracts can create *third-party beneficiaries, assignees,* and *delegates.* These nonparties receive rights from, or have obligations to, one of the contracting parties. They stand in the shoes of the original contractor.

With a third-party beneficiary, one of the contracting parties is bargaining for the benefit of another. In the case of an assignment, one of the parties is transferring a right, such as the receipt of money. In the case of delegation, one of them is transferring an obligation, such as to perform a service. Each element must be analyzed separately.

Occasionally, nonparty rights are excluded from the first-year law school curriculum. The time demands imposed in learning basic contract principles may leave few classes available to tackle third-party beneficiaries, assignments, and delegations. In light of the role of these issues in law school, only an outline of nonparty rights and duties are presented here. However, the basic principles are covered.

EXAMPLE: Johnny contracts to have Santos mow his mom's lawn for $100. Santos, who wants to settle a $100 debt to his own bank, arranges to have the $100 paid directly to it. Also, since Santos becomes too busy with business, he later delegates the mowing to another competent lawnmower.

Mom is a *third-party beneficiary* of the contract; Santos is the *promisor,* because he made a promise for mom's benefit; Johnny is the *promisee,* who received a

> promise from Santos, in order to benefit mom; the $100 was assigned to the bank, which becomes an *assignee;* the mowing was delegated to the other landscaper, who becomes a *delegate.*

I. Third-Party Beneficiaries

West's Key No. Digests, Contracts ☞ 187. (95k187)

A. VESTING

When the third-party claims and rights and duties have been irreversibly established, they are said to have *vested*. A beneficiary's rights vest when she materially changes position in reliance on the promised benefit, sues on the contract, or manifests consent:

- Once rights vest, the original parties can no longer modify or eliminate them.

- At vesting, the accumulated rights and duties have accrued to the original contracting parties, and then flow on to the nonparties. After vesting, any new claims and rights that arise between the contracting parties and/or others remain their own.

- Once rights have vested, they can be enforced by intended beneficiaries.

West's Key No. Digests, Assignments ☞ 1. (38k1)

B. INTENDED BENEFICIARIES

These rights are only enforceable by intended beneficiaries. They must be identified in the contract; the original contracting parties must have purposely benefitted them; and conferring the benefit must fulfill the original contracting party's duty.

West's Key No. Digests, Assignments ☞ 1-30. (38I)

C. INCIDENTAL BENEFICIARIES

Incidental beneficiaries are third parties who unintentionally or inadvertently benefit from a contract, in contrast to intended beneficiaries. They have no enforceable rights.

> **EXAMPLE:** Johnny contracts to have Santos mow his mom's lawn for $100. Santos buys his landscaping supplies at a nearby nursery. Though the nursery would

> benefit from the contract, it is merely an incidental beneficiary with no enforceable rights.

West's Key No. Digests, Assignments ⬥ 31-61. (38II)

D. CREDITOR BENEFICIARIES

A creditor beneficiary receives a benefit to satisfy an existing obligation. This kind of beneficiary may sue either the promisor or the promisee.

> **EXAMPLE:** Johnny contracts with Santos to mow his lawn for $100. Santos, who wants to settle a $100 debt to his bank, includes a provision to pay the $100 directly to the bank. The bank can sue Santos, the promisee (he received the promise to pay the debt from Johnny), or Johnny, the promisor (he made the promise to pay the debt to Santos).
> The parties have several simultaneous relationships, which can make the issue of who is promisor and who is promisee confusing. To the bank, Johnny is the promisor because he promised to pay the debt first owed to Santos. Santos is the promisee, because he received Johnny's promise to pay the bank.

West's Key No. Digests, Assignments ⬥ 54. (38k54)

E. DONEE BENEFICIARIES

A donee beneficiary receives a benefit as a gift. A donee beneficiary may sue only the promisor, since the promisee owes nothing to the beneficiary, unless the promisee induces the donee beneficiary to rely on the promise reasonably, foreseeably, and detrimentally.

> **EXAMPLE:** Johnny contracts to have Santos mow his mom's lawn for $100. Mom can sue Santos, the promisor (he made the promise to mow the lawn), but not Johnny, the promisee, who was making only a gift, not paying an enforceable debt.

West's Key No. Digests, Assignments ⬥ 115. (38k115)

F. ENFORCEMENT SUMMARY

■ 1. Beneficiaries

The beneficiary can enforce the promise against the promisor as it existed at the moment of vesting.

■ 2. Promisee

The promisee can enforce the promise against the promisor if the beneficiary doesn't.

◼ 3. Creditor Beneficiary

A creditor beneficiary can sue the promisor, and still sue the promisee on the original obligation that was to be satisfied by the third-party promise of performance.

◼ 4. Promisor's Defenses

Generally, the promisor may raise any defense against the third-party beneficiary's claims that might have been raised against the promisee, since the beneficiary stands in the shoes of the promisee.

G. SPECIAL CONTRACTS

◼ 1. Government Contracts

If a governmental entity enters into a contract with a private company to provide services for the public, an ordinary citizen will usually not be considered an intended beneficiary.

◼ 2. Suretyship Bonds

Contractors often assure the completion of work. If a contractor obtains a suretyship bond to assure the owner of the contractor's performance, the promise between the contractor and the bonding company creates an intended beneficiary—the owner.

◼ 3. Mortgage Assumptions

When a party buys property, the party is a transferee, because title is transferred to him. If the transferee also assumes an existing mortgage, the lender may foreclose and hold the transferee personally liable for any amount still due on the underlying debt after the foreclosure sale. The lender is considered a third-party beneficiary of the mortgage assumption and may enforce its rights against the transferee, or against the transferor (the original owner).

II. Assignments of Rights

If a party transfers an existing right, it is an assignment. Appointment of another to perform one's duties is a delegation. Assignment of an entire contract is both an assignment of rights and a delegation of duties.

> **EXAMPLE:** A contractor was building an office tower. He and his bank agreed that, in exchange for the bank's lending the contractor $1,000,000, the contractor would have the owner of the tower pay all profits directly to the bank. There has been an assignment of the contractor's rights.

A. DEFINITIONS

■ 1. Obligor

The person who has the obligation to perform under the original contract is called the obligor.

■ 2. Assignor-Obligee

The person who was originally entitled to receive the obligor's performance, and who then assigns it away is termed an assignor-obligee.

■ 3. Assignee

The person who is now entitled to performance as a result of the assignment is the assignee.

■ 4. Assignment

An assignment is an irrevocable, immediate transfer of all or part of an assignor's rights under a contract. A promise to transfer rights in the future is not an assignment.

B. PROHIBITED ASSIGNMENTS

■ 1. Express Terms

Contract prohibition can remove the privilege, but not the right to assign. In other words, a party can always assign a benefit whose assignment of which is prohibited in the contract, but both may then be simultaneously liable for breach of the contract.

Under the UCC, assigning a contract right is always valid (UCC § 2-210).

■ 2. Illegal

Some assignments are prohibited by applicable statute, such as statutes that prohibit the assignment of wages.

■ 3. Increased Burden or Risk

Assignments that would materially increase a burden or risk in the obligor's duty are prohibited. Typically, this occurs in output and requirements contracts, when the assignment makes them unreasonably disproportionate from the original terms (UCC §§ 2-210(5) and 2-609(4)).

> **EXAMPLE:** An insurance company insures a warehouse that an asbestos manufacturer owns. The policy covers loss due to fire. If the asbestos company sells the warehouse to the Greasy Rag Company, he may not assign his rights under the insurance policy without the insurance company's consent.

C. PROCEDURE

The assignor assigns to the assignee the benefit of the performance owed by the obligor, as stated in the contract. A valid assignment must include a description of the right assigned, words of present not future transfer, and a writing, if required. There is an implied warranty of assignability and enforceability. After the assignment has vested, the obligor cannot change the contract terms. Assignments usually need to be in writing for the sale of goods over $500, the lease of goods, interests in real property, wages, or security interests.

D. GRATUITOUS ASSIGNMENTS

A gratuitous assignment is automatically revoked by the death or bankruptcy of the assignor; a new assignment of the same right; or upon notice of termination. However, it can be enforced like an ordinary assignment if an assignee reasonably, foreseeably, and detrimentally relied on the assignment; or if the assignee has a document symbolizing the assignment, such as a stock certificate.

E. MULTIPLE ASSIGNMENTS

■ 1. Revocable

If an assignment is revocable, it is automatically revoked by any subsequent assignment of the same right. The newer assignment is then valid until revoked, made irrevocable, or performed.

■ 2. Irrevocable

If multiple irrevocable assignments are made, the first in time prevails, unless the new assignee paid for the assignment; had a judgment against the obligor; received a symbolic document representing the assignment; or made a new contract with the obligor (*a novation*).

III. Delegation of Duties

As a counterpart to the right of a contracting party to assign a right, a party can often transfer an obligation to perform a duty. The original party whose duty it is to render a performance may transfer this duty to a third person after the contract has been formed. This is referred to as a *delegation of duties*. However, the party delegating still remains liable under the original contract.

> **EXAMPLE:** A farmer contracts to deliver Golden Delicious apples to a grocer on a weekly basis. The farmer then contracts with a fruit distributor to make the deliveries in his stead. The type and quality of the apples is the same. The farmer has successfully *delegated* his duties to the distributor. The grocer will receive the performance due him directly from the distributor.

A. DEFINITIONS

■ 1. Obligee
The party to the original contract entitled to receive the performance which is being delegated is called the obligee. Her permission is sometimes required before the delegation is permitted.

■ 2. Delegant (or Delegator)
The party to the original contract who owes a performance, who then delegates it to a third person is termed the delegant or delegator. After the delegation, the new delegate has the duty to perform, but this original contracting party remains liable for the performance.

■ 3. Delegate
A delegate is the third party to whom the delegator delegates the duty. This person was not a party to the original contract, but agrees to shoulder the contract duty received from the delegant.

B. RULES OF DELEGATION

■ 1. Power to Delegate
An obligee must accept performance by a delegate if the contract duty is delegable. It is self-evident that she need not accept delegation of a nondelegable duty.

■ 2. Guarantee
Even after an effective delegation, the delegant remains liable as a surety to the obligee, under the original contract. The delegant owes a warranty of performance to the original obligee.

■ 3. Consideration
The delegate is not liable for the performance of the delegated duties unless the delegation is for consideration. If the delegation was for consideration, both the obligee and delegate can enforce the performance against the delegatee.

C. PROHIBITED DELEGATIONS

■ 1. Express Terms

Both the right and the privilege to delegate can be completely prohibited in a contract. In that case, any supposed delegation by one party is completely null and void.

■ 2. Illegal

Some delegations are prohibited by applicable statutes, such as one that prohibits lawyers from delegating their work to nonlawyers. Any such supposed delegation is completely null and void.

■ 3. Decreased Value

Delegations that would materially decrease the value of the obligee's rights are prohibited. Typically, this occurs in unique personal services contracts.

> EXAMPLE: A student says to a friend: "I'll sell you my old sports car for $400," and the friend says: "I accept." They draw up and sign a complete, written contract. The student attempts to assign the $400 to her sister to pay a debt already owed. However, the student had originally agreed to take a personal check from the buyer, but the sister insisted upon a cashier's check which would cost more. This is an added burden upon the obligor, and the delegation would be invalid.

APPENDIX A

UCC Excerpts

APPENDIX A: UCC EXCERPTS

§ 1-201. GENERAL DEFINITIONS.

Subject to additional definitions contained in the subsequent Articles of this Act which are applicable to specific Articles or Parts thereof, and unless the context otherwise requires, in this Act:

(1) "Action" in the sense of a judicial proceeding includes recoupment, counterclaim, set-off, suit in equity and any other proceedings in which rights are determined.

(2) "Aggrieved party" means a party entitled to resort to a remedy.

(3) "Agreement" means the bargain of the parties in fact as found in their language or by implication from other circumstances including course of dealing or usage of trade or course of performance as provided in this Act (Sections 1-205 and 2-208). Whether an agreement has legal consequences is determined by the provisions of this Act, if applicable; otherwise by the law of contracts (Section 1-103). (Compare "Contract".)

(4) "Bank" means any person engaged in the business of banking.

(5) "Bearer" means the person in possession of an instrument, document of title, or certificated security payable to bearer or indorsed in blank.

(5) "Bearer" means the person in possession of an instrument, document of title, or security payable to bearer or indorsed in blank.

(6) "Bill of lading" means a document evidencing the receipt of goods for shipment issued by a person engaged in the business of transporting or forwarding goods, and includes an airbill. "Airbill" means a document serving for air transportation as a bill of lading does for marine or rail transportation, and includes an air consignment note or air waybill.

(7) "Branch" includes a separately incorporated foreign branch of a bank.

(8) "Burden of establishing" a fact means the burden of persuading the triers of fact that the existence of the fact is more probable than its non-existence.

(9) "Buyer in ordinary course of business" means a person who in good faith and without knowledge that the sale to him is in violation of the ownership rights or security interest of a third party in the goods buys in ordinary course from a person in the business of selling goods of that kind but does not include a pawnbroker. All persons who sell minerals or the like (including oil and gas) at wellhead or minehead shall be deemed to be persons in the business of selling goods of that kind. "Buying" may be for cash or by exchange of other property or on secured or unsecured credit and includes receiving goods or documents of title

under a pre-existing contract for sale but does not include a transfer in bulk or as security for or in total or partial satisfaction of a money debt.

(9) "Buyer in ordinary course of business" means a person who in good faith and without knowledge that the sale to him is in violation of the ownership rights or security interest of a third party in the goods buys in ordinary course from a person in the business of selling goods of that kind but does not include a pawnbroker. "Buying" may be for cash or by exchange of other property or on secured or unsecured credit and includes receiving goods or documents of title under a pre-existing contract for sale but does not include a transfer in bulk or as security for or in total or partial satisfaction of a money debt.

(10) "Conspicuous": A term or clause is conspicuous when it is so written that a reasonable person against whom it is to operate ought to have noticed it. A printed heading in capitals (as: Non-Negotiable Bill of Lading) is conspicuous. Language in the body of a form is "conspicuous" if it is in larger or other contrasting type or color. But in a telegram any stated term is "conspicuous". Whether a term or clause is "conspicuous" or not is for decision by the court.

(11) "Contract" means the total legal obligation which results from the parties' agreement as affected by this Act and any other applicable rules of law. (Compare "Agreement".)

(12) "Creditor" includes a general creditor, a secured creditor, a lien creditor and any representative of creditors, including an assignee for the benefit of creditors, a trustee in bankruptcy, a receiver in equity and an executor or administrator of an insolvent debtor's or assignor's estate.

(13) "Defendant" includes a person in the position of defendant in a cross-action or counterclaim.

(14) "Delivery" with respect to instruments, documents of title, chattel paper, or certificated securities means voluntary transfer of possession.

(14) "Delivery" with respect to instruments, documents of title, chattel paper or securities means voluntary transfer of possession.

(15) "Document of title" includes bill of lading, dock warrant, dock receipt, warehouse receipt or order for the delivery of goods, and also any other document which in the regular course of business or financing is treated as adequately evidencing that the person in possession of it is entitled to receive, hold, and dispose of the document and the goods it covers. To be a document of title a document must purport to be issued by or addressed to a bailee and purport to cover goods in the bailee's possession which are either identified or are fungible portions of an identified mass.

(16) "Fault" means wrongful act, omission or breach.

(17) "Fungible" with respect to goods or securities means goods or securities of which any unit is, by nature or usage of trade, the equivalent

of any other like unit. Goods which are not fungible shall be deemed fungible for the purposes of this Act to the extent that under a particular agreement or document unlike units are treated as equivalents.

(18) "Genuine" means free of forgery or counterfeiting.

(19) "Good faith" means honesty in fact in the conduct or transaction concerned.

(20) "Holder" means a person who is in possession of a document of title or an instrument or a certificated investment security drawn, issued, or indorsed to him or his order or to bearer or in blank.

(21) To "honor" is to pay or to accept and pay, or where a credit so engages to purchase or discount a draft complying with the terms of the credit.

(22) "Insolvency proceedings" includes any assignment for the benefit of creditors or other proceedings intended to liquidate or rehabilitate the estate of the person involved.

(23) A person is "insolvent" who either has ceased to pay his debts in the ordinary course of business or cannot pay his debts as they become due or is insolvent within the meaning of the federal bankruptcy law.

(24) "Money" means a medium of exchange authorized or adopted by a domestic or foreign government as a part of its currency.

(25) A person has "notice" of a fact when

(a) he has actual knowledge of it; or

(b) he has received a notice or notification of it; or

(c) from all the facts and circumstances known to him at the time in question he has reason to know that it exists.

A person "knows" or has "knowledge" of a fact when he has actual knowledge of it. "Discover" or "learn" or a word or phrase of similar import refers to knowledge rather than to reason to know. The time and circumstances under which a notice or notification may cease to be effective are not determined by this Act.

(26) A person "notifies" or "gives" a notice or notification to another by taking such steps as may be reasonably required to inform the other in ordinary course whether or not such other actually comes to know of it. A person "receives" a notice or notification when

(a) it comes to his attention; or

(b) it is duly delivered at the place of business through which the contract was made or at any other place held out by him as the place for receipt of such communications.

(27) Notice, knowledge or a notice or notification received by an organization is effective for a particular transaction from the time when it is brought to the attention of the individual conducting that transaction, and in any event from the time when it would have been brought to his attention if the organization had exercised due diligence. An organization exercises due diligence if it maintains reasonable routines for

communicating significant information to the person conducting the transaction and there is reasonable compliance with the routines. Due diligence does not require an individual acting for the organization to communicate information unless such communication is part of his regular duties or unless he has reason to know of the transaction and that the transaction would be materially affected by the information.

(28) "Organization" includes a corporation, government or governmental subdivision or agency, business trust, estate, trust, partnership or association, two or more persons having a joint or common interest, or any other legal or commercial entity.

(29) "Party", as distinct from "third party", means a person who has engaged in a transaction or made an agreement within this Act.

(30) "Person" includes an individual or an organization (See Section 1-102).

(31) "Presumption" or "presumed" means that the trier of fact must find the existence of the fact presumed unless and until evidence is introduced which would support a finding of its non-existence.

(32) "Purchase" includes taking by sale, discount, negotiation, mortgage, pledge, lien, issue or re-issue, gift or any other voluntary transaction creating an interest in property.

(33) "Purchaser" means a person who takes by purchase.

(34) "Remedy" means any remedial right to which an aggrieved party is entitled with or without resort to a tribunal.

(35) "Representative" includes an agent, an officer of a corporation or association, and a trustee, executor or administrator of an estate, or any other person empowered to act for another.

(36) "Rights" includes remedies.

(37) "Security interest" means an interest in personal property or fixtures which secures payment or performance of an obligation. The retention or reservation of title by a seller of goods notwithstanding shipment or delivery to the buyer (Section 2-401) is limited in effect to a reservation of a "security interest". The term also includes any interest of a buyer of accounts or chattel paper which is subject to Article 9. The special property interest of a buyer of goods on identification of those goods to a contract for sale under Section 2-401 is not a "security interest", but a buyer may also acquire a "security interest" by complying with Article 9. Unless a consignment is intended as security, reservation of title thereunder is not a "security interest", but a consignment in any event is subject to the provisions on consignment sales (Section 2-326).

Whether a transaction creates a lease or security interest is determined by the facts of each case; however, a transaction creates a security interest if the consideration the lessee is to pay the lessor for the right to possession and use of the goods is an obligation for the term of the lease not subject to termination by the lessee, and

(a) the original term of the lease is equal to or greater than the remaining economic life of the goods,

(b) the lessee is bound to renew the lease for the remaining economic life of the goods or is bound to become the owner of the goods,

(c) the lessee has an option to renew the lease for the remaining economic life of the goods for no additional consideration or nominal additional consideration upon compliance with the lease agreement, or

(d) the lessee has an option to become the owner of the goods for no additional consideration or nominal additional consideration upon compliance with the lease agreement.

A transaction does not create a security interest merely because it provides that

(a) the present value of the consideration the lessee is obligated to pay the lessor for the right to possession and use of the goods is substantially equal to or is greater than the fair market value of the goods at the time the lease is entered into,

(b) the lessee assumes risk of loss of the goods, or agrees to pay taxes, insurance, filing, recording, or registration fees, or service or maintenance costs with respect to the goods,

(c) the lessee has an option to renew the lease or to become the owner of the goods,

(d) the lessee has an option to renew the lease for a fixed rent that is equal to or greater than the reasonably predictable fair market rent for the use of the goods for the term of the renewal at the time the option is to be performed, or

(e) the lessee has an option to become the owner of the goods for a fixed price that is equal to or greater than the reasonably predictable fair market value of the goods at the time the option is to be performed.

For purposes of this subsection (37):

(x) Additional consideration is not nominal if (i) when the option to renew the lease is granted to the lessee the rent is stated to be the fair market rent for the use of the goods for the term of the renewal determined at the time the option is to be performed, or (ii) when the option to become the owner of the goods is granted to the lessee the price is stated to be the fair market value of the goods determined at the time the option is to be performed. Additional consideration is nominal if it is less than the lessee's reasonably predictable cost of performing under the lease agreement if the option is not exercised;

(y) "Reasonably predictable" and "remaining economic life of the goods" are to be determined with reference to the facts and circumstances at the time the transaction is entered into; and

(z) "Present value" means the amount as of a date certain of one or more sums payable in the future, discounted to the date certain. The discount is determined by the interest rate specified by the parties if the rate is not manifestly unreasonable at the time the transaction is entered into; otherwise, the discount is determined by a commercially reasonable rate that takes into account the facts and circumstances of each case at the time the transaction was entered into.

(37) "Security interest" means an interest in personal property or fixtures which secures payment or performance of an obligation. The retention or reservation of title by a seller of goods notwithstanding shipment or delivery to the buyer (Section 2-401) is limited in effect to a reservation of a "security interest". The term also includes any interest of a buyer of accounts or chattel paper which is subject to Article 9. The special property interest of a buyer of goods on identification of such goods to a contract for sale under Section 2-401 is not a "security interest", but a buyer may also acquire a "security interest" by complying with Article 9. Unless a lease or consignment is intended as security, reservation of title thereunder is not a "security interest" but a consignment is in any event subject to the provisions on consignment sales (Section 2-326). Whether a lease is intended as security is to be determined by the facts of each case; however, (a) the inclusion of an option to purchase does not of itself make the lease one intended for security, and (b) an agreement that upon compliance with the terms of the lease the lessee shall become or has the option to become the owner of the property for no additional consideration or for a nominal consideration does make the lease one intended for security.

(37) "Security interest" means an interest in personal property or fixtures which secures payment or performance of an obligation. The retention or reservation of title by a seller of goods notwithstanding shipment or delivery to the buyer (Section 2-401) is limited in effect to a reservation of a "security interest". The term also includes any interest of a buyer of accounts, chattel paper, or contract rights which is subject to Article 9. The special property interest of a buyer of goods on identification of such goods to a contract for sale under Section 2-401 is not a "security interest", but a buyer may also acquire a "security interest", by complying with Article 9. Unless a lease or consignment is intended as security, reservation of title thereunder is not a "security interest" but a consignment is in any event subject to the provisions on consignment sales (Section 2-326). Whether a lease is intended as security is to be determined by the facts of each case; however, (a) the inclusion of an option to purchase does not of itself make the lease one intended for security, and (b) an agreement that upon compliance with the terms of the lease the lessee shall become or has the option to become the owner of the property for no additional consideration or for a nominal consideration does make the lease one intended for security.

(38) "Send" in connection with any writing or notice means to deposit in the mail or deliver for transmission by any other usual means of

communication with postage or cost of transmission provided for and properly addressed and in the case of an instrument to an address specified thereon or otherwise agreed, or if there be none to any address reasonable under the circumstances. The receipt of any writing or notice within the time at which it would have arrived if properly sent has the effect of a proper sending.

(39) "Signed" includes any symbol executed or adopted by a party with present intention to authenticate a writing.

(40) "Surety" includes guarantor.

(41) "Telegram" includes a message transmitted by radio, teletype, cable, any mechanical method of transmission, or the like.

(42) "Term" means that portion of an agreement which relates to a particular matter.

(43) "Unauthorized" signature or indorsement means one made without actual, implied or apparent authority and includes a forgery.

(44) "Value". Except as otherwise provided with respect to negotiable instruments and bank collections (Sections 3-303, 4-208 and 4-209) a person gives "value" for rights if he acquires them

(a) in return for a binding commitment to extend credit or for the extension of immediately available credit whether or not drawn upon and whether or not a chargeback is provided for in the event of difficulties in collection; or

(b) as security for or in total or partial satisfaction of a pre-existing claim; or

(c) by accepting delivery pursuant to a pre-existing contract for purchase; or

(d) generally, in return for any consideration sufficient to support a simple contract.

(45) "Warehouse receipt" means a receipt issued by a person engaged in the business of storing goods for hire.

(46) "Written" or "writing" includes printing, typewriting or any other intentional reduction to tangible form.

§ 1-202. PRIMA FACIE EVIDENCE BY THIRD PARTY DOCUMENTS.

A document in due form purporting to be a bill of lading, policy or certificate of insurance, official weigher's or inspector's certificate, consular invoice, or any other document authorized or required by the contract to be issued by a third party shall be prima facie evidence of its own authenticity and genuineness and of the fact stated in the document by the third party.

§ 1-203. OBLIGATION OF GOOD FAITH.

Every contract or duty within this Act imposes an obligation of good faith in its performance or enforcement.

§ 1-204. TIME; REASONABLE TIME; "SEASONABLY".

(1) Whenever this Act requires any action to be taken within a reasonable time, any time which is not manifestly unreasonable may be fixed by agreement.

(2) What is a reasonable time for taking any action depends on the nature, purpose and circumstances of such action.

(3) An action is taken "seasonably" when it is taken at or within the time agreed or if no time is agreed at or within a reasonable time.

§ 1-205. COURSE OF DEALING AND USAGE OF TRADE.

(1) A course of dealing is a sequence of previous conduct between the parties to a particular transaction which is fairly to be regarded as establishing a common basis of understanding for interpreting their expressions and other conduct.

(2) A usage of trade is any practice or method of dealing having such regularity of observance in a place, vocation or trade as to justify an expectation that it will be observed with respect to the transaction in question. The existence and scope of such a usage are to be proved as facts. If it is established that such a usage is embodied in a written trade code or similar writing the interpretation of the writing is for the court.

(3) A course of dealing between parties and any usage of trade in the vocation or trade in which they are engaged or of which they are or should be aware give particular meaning to and supplement or qualify terms of an agreement.

(4) The express terms of an agreement and an applicable course of dealing or usage of trade shall be construed wherever reasonable as consistent with each other; but when such construction is unreasonable express terms control both course of dealing and usage of trade and course of dealing controls usage of trade.

(5) An applicable usage of trade in the place where any part of performance is to occur shall be used in interpreting the agreement as to that part of the performance.

(6) Evidence of a relevant usage of trade offered by one party is not admissible unless and until he has given the other party such notice as the court finds sufficient to prevent unfair surprise to the latter.

§ 1-206. STATUTE OF FRAUDS FOR KINDS OF PERSONAL PROPERTY NOT OTHERWISE COVERED.

(1) Except in the cases described in subsection (2) of this section a contract for the sale of personal property is not enforceable by way of action or defense beyond five thousand dollars in amount or value of remedy unless there is some writing which indicates that a contract for sale has been made between the parties at a defined or stated price,

reasonably identifies the subject matter, and is signed by the party against whom enforcement is sought or by his authorized agent.

§ 1-207. PERFORMANCE OR ACCEPTANCE UNDER RESERVATION OF RIGHTS.
(1) A party who, with explicit reservation of rights, performs or promises performance or assents to performance in a manner demanded or offered by the other party does not thereby prejudice the rights reserved. Such words as "without prejudice", "under protest" or the like are sufficient.
  (2) Subsection (1) does not apply to an accord and satisfaction.

§ 1-208. OPTION TO ACCELERATE AT WILL.
A term providing that one party or his successor in interest may accelerate payment or performance or require collateral or additional collateral "at will" or "when he deems himself insecure" or in words of similar import shall be construed to mean that he shall have power to do so only if he in good faith believes that the prospect of payment or performance is impaired. The burden of establishing lack of good faith is on the party against whom the power has been exercised.

§ 1-209. SUBORDINATED OBLIGATIONS.
An obligation may be issued as subordinated to payment of another obligation of the person obligated, or a creditor may subordinate his right to payment of an obligation by agreement with either the person obligated or another creditor of the person obligated. Such a subordination does not create a security interest as against either the common debtor or a subordinated creditor. This section shall be construed as declaring the law as it existed prior to the enactment of this section and not as modifying it. Added 1966.

§ 2-201. FORMAL REQUIREMENTS; STATUTE OF FRAUDS.
(1) Except as otherwise provided in this section a contract for the sale of goods for the price of $500 or more is not enforceable by way of action or defense unless there is some writing sufficient to indicate that a contract for sale has been made between the parties and signed by the party against whom enforcement is sought or by his authorized agent or broker. A writing is not insufficient because it omits or incorrectly states a term agreed upon but the contract is not enforceable under this paragraph beyond the quantity of goods shown in such writing.
  (2) Between merchants if within a reasonable time a writing in confirmation of the contract and sufficient against the sender is received and the party receiving it has reason to know its contents, it satisfies the requirements of subsection (1) against such party unless written notice of objection to its contents is given within 10 days after it is received.

(3) A contract which does not satisfy the requirements of subsection (1) but which is valid in other respects is enforceable

(a) if the goods are to be specially manufactured for the buyer and are not suitable for sale to others in the ordinary course of the seller's business and the seller, before notice of repudiation is received and under circumstances which reasonably indicate that the goods are for the buyer, has made either a substantial beginning of their manufacture or commitments for their procurement; or

(b) if the party against whom enforcement is sought admits in his pleading, testimony or otherwise in court that a contract for sale was made, but the contract is not enforceable under this provision beyond the quantity of goods admitted; or

(c) with respect to goods for which payment has been made and accepted or which have been received and accepted (Sec. 2-606).

§ 2-202. FINAL WRITTEN EXPRESSION: PAROL OR EXTRINSIC EVIDENCE.

Terms with respect to which the confirmatory memoranda of the parties agree or which are otherwise set forth in a writing intended by the parties as a final expression of their agreement with respect to such terms as are included therein may not be contradicted by evidence of any prior agreement or of a contemporaneous oral agreement but may be explained or supplemented

(a) by course of dealing or usage of trade (Section 1-205) or by course of performance (Section 2-208); and

(b) by evidence of consistent additional terms unless the court finds the writing to have been intended also as a complete and exclusive statement of the terms of the agreement.

§ 2-203. SEALS INOPERATIVE.

The affixing of a seal to a writing evidencing a contract for sale or an offer to buy or sell goods does not constitute the writing of a sealed instrument and the law with respect to sealed instruments does not apply to such a contract or offer.

§ 2-204. FORMATION IN GENERAL.

(1) A contract for sale of goods may be made in any manner sufficient to show agreement, including conduct by both parties which recognizes the existence of such a contract.

(2) An agreement sufficient to constitute a contract for sale may be found even though the moment of its making is undetermined.

(3) Even though one or more terms are left open a contract for sale does not fail for indefiniteness if the parties have intended to make a contract and there is a reasonably certain basis for giving an appropriate remedy.

§ 2-205. FIRM OFFERS.

An offer by a merchant to buy or sell goods in a signed writing which by its terms give assurance that it will be held open is not revocable, for lack of consideration, during the time stated or if no time is stated for a reasonable time, but in no event may such period of irrevocability exceed three months; but any such term of assurance on a form supplied by the offeree must be separately signed by the offeror.

§ 2-206. OFFER AND ACCEPTANCE IN FORMATION OF CONTRACT.

(1) Unless otherwise unambiguously indicated by the language or circumstances

(a) an offer to make a contract shall be construed as inviting acceptance in any manner and by any medium reasonable in the circumstances;

(b) an order or other offer to buy goods for prompt or current shipment shall be construed as inviting acceptance either by a prompt promise to ship or by the prompt or current shipment of conforming or non-conforming goods, but such a shipment of non-conforming goods does not constitute an acceptance if the seller seasonably notifies the buyer that the shipment is offered only as an accommodation to the buyer.

(2) Where the beginning of a requested performance is a reasonable mode of acceptance an offeror who is not notified of acceptance within a reasonable time may treat the offer as having lapsed before acceptance.

§ 2-207. ADDITIONAL TERMS IN ACCEPTANCE OR CONFIRMATION.

(1) A definite and seasonable expression of acceptance or a written confirmation which is sent within a reasonable time operates as an acceptance even though it states terms additional to or different from those offered or agreed upon, unless acceptance is expressly made conditional on assent to the additional or different terms.

(2) The additional terms are to be construed as proposals for addition to the contract. Between merchants such terms become part of the contract unless:

(a) the offer expressly limits acceptance to the terms of the offer;

(b) they materially alter it; or

(c) notification of objection to them has already been given or is given within a reasonable time after notice of them is received.

(3) Conduct by both parties which recognizes the existence of a contract is sufficient to establish a contract for sale although the writings of the parties do not otherwise establish a contract. In such case the terms of the particular contract consist of those terms on which the writings of the parties agree, together with any supplementary terms incorporated under any other provisions of this Act.

§ 2-208. COURSE OF PERFORMANCE OR PRACTICAL CONSTRUCTION.

(1) Where the contract for sale involves repeated occasions for performance by either party with knowledge of the nature of the performance and opportunity for objection to it by the other, any course of performance accepted or acquiesced in without objection shall be relevant to determine the meaning of the agreement.

(2) The express terms of the agreement and any such course of performance, as well as any course of dealing and usage of trade, shall be construed whenever reasonable as consistent with each other; but when such construction is unreasonable, express terms shall control course of performance and course of performance shall control both course of dealing and usage of trade (Section 1-205).

(3) Subject to the provisions of the next section on modification and waiver, such course of performance shall be relevant to show a waiver or modification of any term inconsistent with such course of performance.

§ 2-209. MODIFICATION, RESCISSION AND WAIVER.

(1) An agreement modifying a contract within this Article needs no consideration to be binding.

(2) A signed agreement which excludes modification or rescission except by a signed writing cannot be otherwise modified or rescinded, but except as between merchants such a requirement on a form supplied by the merchant must be separately signed by the other party.

(3) The requirements of the statute of frauds section of this Article (Section 2-201) must be satisfied if the contract as modified is within its provisions.

(4) Although an attempt at modification or rescission does not satisfy the requirements of subsection (2) or (3) it can operate as a waiver.

(5) A party who has made a waiver affecting an executory portion of the contract may retract the waiver by reasonable notification received by the other party that strict performance will be required of any term waived, unless the retraction would be unjust in view of a material change of position in reliance on the waiver.

§ 2-210. DELEGATION OF PERFORMANCE; ASSIGNMENT OF RIGHTS.

(1) A party may perform his duty through a delegate unless otherwise agreed or unless the other party has a substantial interest in having his original promisor perform or control the acts required by the contract. No delegation of performance relieves the party delegating of any duty to perform or any liability for breach.

(2) Unless otherwise agreed all rights of either seller or buyer can be assigned except where the assignment would materially change the duty of the other party, or increase materially the burden or risk imposed on

him by his contract, or impair materially his chance of obtaining return performance. A right to damages for breach of the whole contract or a right arising out of the assignor's due performance of his entire obligation can be assigned despite agreement otherwise.

(3) Unless the circumstances indicate the contrary a prohibition of assignment of "the contract" is to be construed as barring only the delegation to the assignee of the assignor's performance.

(4) An assignment of "the contract" or of "all my rights under the contract" or an assignment in similar general terms is an assignment of rights and unless the language or the circumstances (as in an assignment for security) indicate the contrary, it is a delegation of performance of the duties of the assignor and its acceptance by the assignee constitutes a promise by him to perform those duties. This promise is enforceable by either the assignor or the other party to the original contract.

(5) The other party may treat any assignment which delegates performance as creating reasonable grounds for insecurity and may without prejudice to his rights against the assignor demand assurances from the assignee (Section 2-609).

§ 2-301. GENERAL OBLIGATIONS OF PARTIES.
The obligation of the seller is to transfer and deliver and that of the buyer is to accept and pay in accordance with the contract.

§ 2-302. UNCONSCIONABLE CONTRACT OR CLAUSE.
(1) If the court as a matter of law finds the contract or any clause of the contract to have been unconscionable at the time it was made the court may refuse to enforce the contract, or it may enforce the remainder of the contract without the unconscionable clause, or it may so limit the application of any unconscionable clause as to avoid any unconscionable result.

(2) When it is claimed or appears to the court that the contract or any clause thereof may be unconscionable the parties shall be afforded a reasonable opportunity to present evidence as to its commercial setting, purpose and effect to aid the court in making the determination.

§ 2-303. ALLOCATION OR DIVISION OF RISKS.
Where this Article allocates a risk or a burden as between the parties-"unless otherwise agreed", the agreement may not only shift the allocation but may also divide the risk or burden.

§ 2-304. PRICE PAYABLE IN MONEY, GOODS, REALTY, OR OTHERWISE.
(1) The price can be made payable in money or otherwise. If it is payable in whole or in part in goods each party is a seller of the goods which he is to transfer.

(2) Even though all or part of the price is payable in an interest in realty the transfer of the goods and the seller's obligations with reference to them are subject to this Article, but not the transfer of the interest in realty or the transferor's obligations in connection therewith.

§ 2-305. OPEN PRICE TERM.

(1) The parties if they so intend can conclude a contract for sale even though the price is not settled. In such a case the price is a reasonable price at the time for delivery if

(a) nothing is said as to price; or

(b) the price is left to be agreed by the parties and they fail to agree; or

(c) the price is to be fixed in terms of some agreed market or other standard as set or recorded by a third person or agency and it is not so set or recorded.

(2) A price to be fixed by the seller or by the buyer means a price for him to fix in good faith.

(3) When a price left to be fixed otherwise than by agreement of the parties fails to be fixed through fault of one party the other may at his option treat the contract as cancelled or himself fix a reasonable price.

(4) Where, however, the parties intend not to be bound unless the price be fixed or agreed and it is not fixed or agreed there is no contract. In such a case the buyer must return any goods already received or if unable so to do must pay their reasonable value at the time of delivery and the seller must return any portion of the price paid on account.

§ 2-306. OUTPUT, REQUIREMENTS AND EXCLUSIVE DEALINGS.

(1) A term which measures the quantity by the output of the seller or the requirements of the buyer means such actual output or requirements as may occur in good faith, except that no quantity unreasonably dispro-portionate to any stated estimate or in the absence of a stated estimate to any normal or otherwise comparable prior output or requirements may be tendered or demanded.

(2) A lawful agreement by either the seller or the buyer for exclusive dealing in the kind of goods concerned imposes unless otherwise agreed an obligation by the seller to use best efforts to supply the goods and by the buyer to use best efforts to promote their sale.

§ 2-307. DELIVERY IN SINGLE LOT OR SEVERAL LOTS.

Unless otherwise agreed all goods called for by a contract for sale must be tendered in a single delivery and payment is due only on such tender but where the circumstances give either party the right to make or demand delivery in lots the price if it can be apportioned may be demanded for each lot.

§ 2-308. ABSENCE OF SPECIFIED PLACE FOR DELIVERY.

Unless otherwise agreed

(a) the place for delivery of goods is the seller's place of business or if he has none his residence; but

(b) in a contract for sale of identified goods which to the knowledge of the parties at the time of contracting are in some other place, that place is the place for their delivery; and

(c) documents of title may be delivered through customary banking channels.

§ 2-309. ABSENCE OF SPECIFIC TIME PROVISIONS; NOTICE OF TERMINATION.

(1) The time for shipment or delivery or any other action under a contract if not provided in this Article or agreed upon shall be a reasonable time.

(2) Where the contract provides for successive performances but is indefinite in duration it is valid for a reasonable time but unless otherwise agreed may be terminated at any time by either party.

(3) Termination of a contract by one party except on the happening of an agreed event requires that reasonable notification be received by the other party and an agreement dispensing with notification is invalid if its operation would be unconscionable.

§ 2-310. OPEN TIME FOR PAYMENT OR RUNNING OF CREDIT; AUTHORITY TO SHIP UNDER RESERVATION.

Unless otherwise agreed

(a) payment is due at the time and place at which the buyer is to receive the goods even though the place of shipment is the place of delivery; and

(b) if the seller is authorized to send the goods he may ship them under reservation, and may tender the documents of title, but the buyer may inspect the goods after their arrival before payment is due unless such inspection is inconsistent with the terms of the contract (Section 2-513); and

(c) if delivery is authorized and made by way of documents of title otherwise than by subsection (b) then payment is due at the time and place at which the buyer is to receive the documents regardless of where the goods are to be received; and

(d) where the seller is required or authorized to ship the goods on credit the credit period runs from the time of shipment but post-dating the invoice or delaying its dispatch will correspondingly delay the starting of the credit period.

§ 2-311. OPTIONS AND COOPERATION RESPECTING PERFORMANCE.

(1) An agreement for sale which is otherwise sufficiently definite (subsection (3) of Section 2-204) to be a contract is not made invalid by the fact

that it leaves particulars of performance to be specified by one of the parties. Any such specification must be made in good faith and within limits set by commercial reasonableness.

(2) Unless otherwise agreed specifications relating to assortment of the goods are at the buyer's option and except as otherwise provided in subsections (1)(c) and (3) of Section 2-319 specifications or arrangements relating to shipment are at the seller's option.

(3) Where such specification would materially affect the other party's performance but is not seasonably made or where one party's cooperation is necessary to the agreed performance of the other but is not seasonably forthcoming, the other party in addition to all other remedies

(a) is excused for any resulting delay in his own performance; and

(b) may also either proceed to perform in any reasonable manner or after the time for a material part of his own performance treat the failure to specify or to cooperate as a breach by failure to deliver or accept the goods.

§ 2-312. WARRANTY OF TITLE AND AGAINST INFRINGEMENT; BUYER'S OBLIGATION AGAINST INFRINGEMENT.

(1) Subject to subsection (2) there is in a contract for sale a warranty by the seller that

(a) the title conveyed shall be good, and its transfer rightful; and

(b) the goods shall be delivered free from any security interest or other lien or encumbrance of which the buyer at the time of contracting has no knowledge.

(2) A warranty under subsection (1) will be excluded or modified only by specific language or by circumstances which give the buyer reason to know that the person selling does not claim title in himself or that he is purporting to sell only such right or title as he or a third person may have.

(3) Unless otherwise agreed a seller who is a merchant regularly dealing in goods of the kind warrants that the goods shall be delivered free of the rightful claim of any third person by way of infringement or the like but a buyer who furnishes specifications to the seller must hold the seller harmless against any such claim which arises out of compliance with the specifications.

§ 2-313. EXPRESS WARRANTIES BY AFFIRMATION, PROMISE, DESCRIPTION, SAMPLE.

(1) Express warranties by the seller are created as follows:

(a) Any affirmation of fact or promise made by the seller to the buyer which relates to the goods and becomes part of the basis of the bargain creates an express warranty that the goods shall conform to the affirmation or promise.

(b) Any description of the goods which is made part of the basis of the bargain creates an express warranty that the goods shall conform to the description.

(c) Any sample or model which is made part of the basis of the bargain creates an express warranty that the whole of the goods shall conform to the sample or model.

(2) It is not necessary to the creation of an express warranty that the seller use formal words such as "warrant" or "guarantee" or that he have a specific intention to make a warranty, but an affirmation merely of the value of the goods or a statement purporting to be merely the seller's opinion or commendation of the goods does not create a warranty.

§ 2-314. IMPLIED WARRANTY: MERCHANTABILITY; USAGE OF TRADE.

(1) Unless excluded or modified (Section 2-316), a warranty that the goods shall be merchantable is implied in a contract for their sale if the seller is a merchant with respect to goods of that kind. Under this section the serving for value of food or drink to be consumed either on the premises or elsewhere is a sale.

(2) Goods to be merchantable must be at least such as

(a) pass without objection in the trade under the contract description; and

(b) in the case of fungible goods, are of fair average quality within the description; and

(c) are fit for the ordinary purposes for which such goods are used; and

(d) run, within the variations permitted by the agreement, of even kind, quality and quantity within each unit and among all units involved; and

(e) are adequately contained, packaged, and labeled as the agreement may require; and

(f) conform to the promises or affirmations of fact made on the container or label if any.

(3) Unless excluded or modified (Section 2-316) other implied warranties may arise from course of dealing or usage of trade.

§ 2-315. IMPLIED WARRANTY: FITNESS FOR PARTICULAR PURPOSE.

Where the seller at the time of contracting has reason to know any particular purpose for which the goods are required and that the buyer is relying on the seller's skill or judgment to select or furnish suitable goods, there is unless excluded or modified under the next section an implied warranty that the goods shall be fit for such purpose.

§ 2-316. EXCLUSION OR MODIFICATION OF WARRANTIES.

(1) Words or conduct relevant to the creation of an express warranty and words or conduct tending to negate or limit warranty shall be construed

wherever reasonable as consistent with each other; but subject to the provisions of this Article on parol or extrinsic evidence (Section 2-202) negation or limitation is inoperative to the extent that such construction is unreasonable.

(2) Subject to subsection (3), to exclude or modify the implied warranty of merchantability or any part of it the language must mention merchantability and in case of a writing must be conspicuous, and to exclude or modify any implied warranty of fitness the exclusion must be by a writing and conspicuous. Language to exclude all implied warranties of fitness is sufficient if it states, for example, that "There are no warranties which extend beyond the description on the face hereof."

(3) Notwithstanding subsection (2)

(a) unless the circumstances indicate otherwise, all implied warranties are excluded by expressions like "as is", "with all faults" or other language which in common understanding calls the buyer's attention to the exclusion of warranties and makes plain that there is no implied warranty; and

(b) when the buyer before entering into the contract has examined the goods or the sample or model as fully as he desired or has refused to examine the goods there is no implied warranty with regard to defects which an examination ought in the circumstances to have revealed to him; and

(c) an implied warranty can also be excluded or modified by course of dealing or course of performance or usage of trade.

(4) Remedies for breach of warranty can be limited in accordance with the provisions of this Article on liquidation or limitation of damages and on contractual modification of remedy (Sections 2-718 and 2-719).

§ 2-317. CUMULATION AND CONFLICT OF WARRANTIES EXPRESS OR IMPLIED.

Warranties whether express or implied shall be construed as consistent with each other and as cumulative, but if such construction is unreasonable the intention of the parties shall determine which warranty is dominant. In ascertaining that intention the following rules apply:

(a) Exact or technical specifications displace an inconsistent sample or model or general language of description.

(b) A sample from an existing bulk displaces inconsistent general language of description.

(c) Express warranties displace inconsistent implied warranties other than an implied warranty of fitness for a particular purpose.

§ 2-318. THIRD PARTY BENEFICIARIES OF WARRANTIES EXPRESS OR IMPLIED.

Alternative A

A seller's warranty whether express or implied extends to any natural person who is in the family or household of his buyer or who is a guest in his home if it is reasonable to expect that such person may use, consume or be affected by the goods and who is injured in person by breach of the warranty. A seller may not exclude or limit the operation of this section.

Alternative B

A seller's warranty whether express or implied extends to any natural person who may reasonably be expected to use, consume or be affected by the goods and who is injured in person by breach of the warranty. A seller may not exclude or limit the operation of this section.

Alternative C

A seller's warranty whether express or implied extends to any person who may reasonably be expected to use, consume or be affected by the goods and who is injured by breach of the warranty. A seller may not exclude or limit the operation of this section with respect to injury to the person of an individual to whom the warranty extends. As amended 1966.

§ 2-319. F.O.B. AND F.A.S. TERMS.

(1) Unless otherwise agreed the term F.O.B. (which means "free on board") at a named place, even though used only in connection with the stated price, is a delivery term under which

(a) when the term is F.O.B. the place of shipment, the seller must at that place ship the goods in the manner provided in this Article (Section 2-504) and bear the expense and risk of putting them into the possession of the carrier; or

(b) when the term is F.O.B. the place of destination, the seller must at his own expense and risk transport the goods to that place and there tender delivery of them in the manner provided in this Article (Section 2-503);

(c) when under either (a) or (b) the term is also F.O.B. vessel, car or other vehicle, the seller must in addition at his own expense and risk load the goods on board. If the term is F.O.B. vessel the buyer must name the vessel and in an appropriate case the seller must comply with the provisions of this Article on the form of bill of lading (Section 2-323).

(2) Unless otherwise agreed the term F.A.S. vessel (which means "free alongside") at a named port, even though used only in connection with the stated price, is a delivery term under which the seller must

(a) at his own expense and risk deliver the goods alongside the vessel in the manner usual in that port or on a dock designated and provided by the buyer; and

(b) obtain and tender a receipt for the goods in exchange for which the carrier is under a duty to issue a bill of lading.

(3) Unless otherwise agreed in any case falling within subsection (1)(a) or (c) or subsection (2) the buyer must seasonably give any needed

instructions for making delivery, including when the term is F.A.S. or F.O.B. the loading berth of the vessel and in an appropriate case its name and sailing date. The seller may treat the failure of needed instructions as a failure of cooperation under this Article (Section 2-311). He may also at his option move the goods in any reasonable manner preparatory to delivery or shipment.

(4) Under the term F.O.B. vessel or F.A.S. unless otherwise agreed the buyer must make payment against tender of the required documents and the seller may not tender nor the buyer demand delivery of the goods in substitution for the documents.

§ 2-320. C.I.F. AND C. & F. TERMS.

(1) The term C.I.F. means that the price includes in a lump sum the cost of the goods and the insurance and freight to the named destination. The term C. & F. or C.F. means that the price so includes cost and freight to the named destination.

(2) Unless otherwise agreed and even though used only in connection with the stated price and destination, the term C.I.F. destination or its equivalent requires the seller at his own expense and risk to

(a) put the goods into the possession of a carrier at the port for shipment and obtain a negotiable bill or bills of lading covering the entire transportation to the named destination; and

(b) load the goods and obtain a receipt from the carrier (which may be contained in the bill of lading) showing that the freight has been paid or provided for; and

(c) obtain a policy or certificate of insurance, including any war risk insurance, of a kind and on terms then current at the port of shipment in the usual amount, in the currency of the contract, shown to cover the same goods covered by the bill of lading and providing for payment of loss to the order of the buyer or for the account of whom it may concern; but the seller may add to the price the amount of the premium for any such war risk insurance; and

(d) prepare an invoice of the goods and procure any other documents required to effect shipment or to comply with the contract; and

(e) forward and tender with commercial promptness all the documents in due form and with any indorsement necessary to perfect the buyer's rights.

(3) Unless otherwise agreed the term C. & F. or its equivalent has the same effect and imposes upon the seller the same obligations and risks as a C.I.F. term except the obligation as to insurance.

(4) Under the term C.I.F. or C. & F. unless otherwise agreed the buyer must make payment against tender of the required documents and the seller may not tender nor the buyer demand delivery of the goods in substitution for the documents.

§ 2-321. C.I.F. OR C. & F.: "NET LANDED WEIGHTS"; "PAYMENT ON ARRIVAL"; WARRANTY OF CONDITION ON ARRIVAL.

Under a contract containing a term C.I.F. or C. & F.

(1) Where the price is based on or is to be adjusted according to "net landed weights", "delivered weights", "out turn" quantity or quality or the like, unless otherwise agreed the seller must reasonably estimate the price. The payment due on tender of the documents called for by the contract is the amount so estimated, but after final adjustment of the price a settlement must be made with commercial promptness.

(2) An agreement described in subsection (1) or any warranty of quality or condition of the goods on arrival places upon the seller the risk of ordinary deterioration, shrinkage and the like in transportation but has no effect on the place or time of identification to the contract for sale or delivery or on the passing of the risk of loss.

(3) Unless otherwise agreed where the contract provides for payment on or after arrival of the goods the seller must before payment allow such preliminary inspection as is feasible; but if the goods are lost delivery of the documents and payment are due when the goods should have arrived.

§ 2-322. DELIVERY "EX-SHIP".

(1) Unless otherwise agreed a term for delivery of goods "ex-ship" (which means from the carrying vessel) or in equivalent language is not restricted to a particular ship and requires delivery from a ship which has reached a place at the named port of destination where goods of the kind are usually discharged.

(2) Under such a term unless otherwise agreed

(a) the seller must discharge all liens arising out of the carriage and furnish the buyer with a direction which puts the carrier under a duty to deliver the goods; and

(b) the risk of loss does not pass to the buyer until the goods leave the ship's tackle or are otherwise properly unloaded.

§ 2-323. FORM OF BILL OF LADING REQUIRED IN OVERSEAS SHIPMENT; "OVERSEAS".

(1) Where the contract contemplates overseas shipment and contains a term C.I.F. or C. & F. or F.O.B. vessel, the seller unless otherwise agreed must obtain a negotiable bill of lading stating that the goods have been loaded on board or, in the case of a term C.I.F. or C. & F., received for shipment.

(2) Where in a case within subsection (1) a bill of lading has been issued in a set of parts, unless otherwise agreed if the documents are not to be sent from abroad the buyer may demand tender of the full set; otherwise only one part of the bill of lading need be tendered. Even if the agreement expressly requires a full set

(a) due tender of a single part is acceptable within the provisions of this Article on cure of improper delivery (subsection (1) of Section 2-508); and

(b) even though the full set is demanded, if the documents are sent from abroad the person tendering an incomplete set may nevertheless require payment upon furnishing an indemnity which the buyer in good faith deems adequate.

(3) A shipment by water or by air or a contract contemplating such shipment is "overseas" insofar as by usage of trade or agreement it is subject to the commercial, financing or shipping practices characteristic of international deep water commerce.

§ 2-324. "NO ARRIVAL, NO SALE" TERM.

Under a term "no arrival, no sale" or terms of like meaning, unless otherwise agreed,

(a) the seller must properly ship conforming goods and if they arrive by any means he must tender them on arrival but he assumes no obligation that the goods will arrive unless he has caused the non-arrival; and

(b) where without fault of the seller the goods are in part lost or have so deteriorated as no longer to conform to the contract or arrive after the contract time, the buyer may proceed as if there had been casualty to identified goods (Section 2-613).

§ 2-325. "LETTER OF CREDIT" TERM; "CONFIRMED CREDIT".

(1) Failure of the buyer seasonably to furnish an agreed letter of credit is a breach of the contract for sale.

(2) The delivery to seller of a proper letter of credit suspends the buyer's obligation to pay. If the letter of credit is dishonored, the seller may on seasonable notification to the buyer require payment directly from him.

(3) Unless otherwise agreed the term "letter of credit" or "banker's credit" in a contract for sale means an irrevocable credit issued by a financing agency of good repute and, where the shipment is overseas, of good international repute. The term "confirmed credit" means that the credit must also carry the direct obligation of such an agency which does business in the seller's financial market.

§ 2-326. SALE ON APPROVAL AND SALE OR RETURN; CONSIGNMENT SALES AND RIGHTS OF CREDITORS.

(1) Unless otherwise agreed, if delivered goods may be returned by the buyer even though they conform to the contract, the transaction is

(a) a "sale on approval" if the goods are delivered primarily for use, and

(b) a "sale or return" if the goods are delivered primarily for resale.

(2) Except as provided in subsection (3), goods held on approval are not subject to the claims of the buyer's creditors until acceptance; goods

held on sale or return are subject to such claims while in the buyer's possession.

(3) Where goods are delivered to a person for sale and such person maintains a place of business at which he deals in goods of the kind involved, under a name other than the name of the person making delivery, then with respect to claims of creditors of the person conducting the business the goods are deemed to be on sale or return. The provisions of this subsection are applicable even though an agreement purports to reserve title to the person making delivery until payment or resale or uses such words as "on consignment" or "on memorandum". However, this subsection is not applicable if the person making delivery

(a) complies with an applicable law providing for a consignor's interest or the like to be evidenced by a sign, or

(b) establishes that the person conducting the business is generally known by his creditors to be substantially engaged in selling the goods of others, or

(c) complies with the filing provisions of the Article on Secured Transactions (Article 9).

(4) Any "or return" term of a contract for sale is to be treated as a separate contract for sale within the statute of frauds section of this Article (Section 2-201) and as contradicting the sale aspect of the contract within the provisions of this Article on parol or extrinsic evidence (Section 2-202).

§ 2-327. SPECIAL INCIDENTS OF SALE ON APPROVAL AND SALE OR RETURN.

(1) Under a sale on approval unless otherwise agreed

(a) although the goods are identified to the contract the risk of loss and the title do not pass to the buyer until acceptance; and

(b) use of the goods consistent with the purpose of trial is not acceptance but failure seasonably to notify the seller of election to return the goods is acceptance, and if the goods conform to the contract acceptance of any part is acceptance of the whole; and

(c) after due notification of election to return, the return is at the seller's risk and expense but a merchant buyer must follow any reasonable instructions.

(2) Under a sale or return unless otherwise agreed

(a) the option to return extends to the whole or any commercial unit of the goods while in substantially their original condition, but must be exercised seasonably; and

(b) the return is at the buyer's risk and expense.

§ 2-328. SALE BY AUCTION.

(1) In a sale by auction if goods are put up in lots each lot is the subject of a separate sale.

(2) A sale by auction is complete when the auctioneer so announces by the fall of the hammer or in other customary manner. Where a bid is made while the hammer is falling in acceptance of a prior bid the auctioneer may in his discretion reopen the bidding or declare the goods sold under the bid on which the hammer was falling.

(3) Such a sale is with reserve unless the goods are in explicit terms put up without reserve. In an auction with reserve the auctioneer may withdraw the goods at any time until he announces completion of the sale. In an auction without reserve, after the auctioneer calls for bids on an article or lot, that article or lot cannot be withdrawn unless no bid is made within a reasonable time. In either case a bidder may retract his bid until the auctioneer's announcement of completion of the sale, but a bidder's retraction does not revive any previous bid.

(4) If the auctioneer knowingly receives a bid on the seller's behalf or the seller makes or procures such a bid, and notice has not been given that liberty for such bidding is reserved, the buyer may at his option avoid the sale or take the goods at the price of the last good faith bid prior to the completion of the sale. This subsection shall not apply to any bid at a forced sale.

§ 2-401. PASSING OF TITLE; RESERVATION FOR SECURITY; LIMITED APPLICATION OF THIS SECTION.

Each provision of this Article with regard to the rights, obligations and remedies of the seller, the buyer, purchasers or other third parties applies irrespective of title to the goods except where the provision refers to such title. Insofar as situations are not covered by the other provisions of this Article and matters concerning title become material the following rules apply:

(1) Title to goods cannot pass under a contract for sale prior to their identification to the contract (Section 2-501), and unless otherwise explicitly agreed the buyer acquires by their identification a special property as limited by this Act. Any retention or reservation by the seller of the title (property) in goods shipped or delivered to the buyer is limited in effect to a reservation of a security interest. Subject to these provisions and to the provisions of the Article on Secured Transactions (Article 9), title to goods passes from the seller to the buyer in any manner and on any conditions explicitly agreed on by the parties.

(2) Unless otherwise explicitly agreed title passes to the buyer at the time and place at which the seller completes his performance with reference to the physical delivery of the goods, despite any reservation of a security interest and even though a document of title is to be delivered at a different time or place; and in particular and despite any reservation of a security interest by the bill of lading

(a) if the contract requires or authorizes the seller to send the goods to the buyer but does not require him to deliver them at destination, title passes to the buyer at the time and place of shipment; but

(b) if the contract requires delivery at destination, title passes on tender there.

(3) Unless otherwise explicitly agreed where delivery is to be made without moving the goods,

(a) if the seller is to deliver a document of title, title passes at the time when and the place where he delivers such documents; or

(b) if the goods are at the time of contracting already identified and no documents are to be delivered, title passes at the time and place of contracting.

(4) A rejection or other refusal by the buyer to receive or retain the goods, whether or not justified, or a justified revocation of acceptance revests title to the goods in the seller. Such revesting occurs by operation of law and is not a "sale".

§ 2-402. RIGHTS OF SELLER'S CREDITORS AGAINST SOLD GOODS.

(1) Except as provided in subsections (2) and (3), rights of unsecured creditors of the seller with respect to goods which have been identified to a contract for sale are subject to the buyer's rights to recover the goods under this Article (Sections 2-502 and 2-716).

(2) A creditor of the seller may treat a sale or an identification of goods to a contract for sale as void if as against him a retention of possession by the seller is fraudulent under any rule of law of the state where the goods are situated, except that retention of possession in good faith and current course of trade by a merchant-seller for a commercially reasonable time after a sale or identification is not fraudulent.

(3) Nothing in this Article shall be deemed to impair the rights of creditors of the seller

(a) under the provisions of the Article on Secured Transactions (Article 9); or

(b) where identification to the contract or delivery is made not in current course of trade but in satisfaction of or as security for a pre-existing claim for money, security or the like and is made under circumstances which under any rule of law of the state where the goods are situated would apart from this Article constitute the transaction a fraudulent transfer or voidable preference.

§ 2-403. POWER TO TRANSFER; GOOD FAITH PURCHASE OF GOODS; "ENTRUSTING".

(1) A purchaser of goods acquires all title which his transferor had or had power to transfer except that a purchaser of a limited interest acquires

rights only to the extent of the interest purchased. A person with voidable title has power to transfer a good title to a good faith purchaser for value. When goods have been delivered under a transaction of purchase the purchaser has such power even though

(a) the transferor was deceived as to the identity of the purchaser, or

(b) the delivery was in exchange for a check which is later dishonored, or

(c) it was agreed that the transaction was to be a "cash sale", or

(d) the delivery was procured through fraud punishable as larcenous under the criminal law.

(2) Any entrusting of possession of goods to a merchant who deals in goods of that kind gives him power to transfer all rights of the entruster to a buyer in ordinary course of business.

(3) "Entrusting" includes any delivery and any acquiescence in retention of possession regardless of any condition expressed between the parties to the delivery or acquiescence and regardless of whether the procurement of the entrusting or the possessor's disposition of the goods have been such as to be larcenous under the criminal law.

§ 2-501. INSURABLE INTEREST IN GOODS; MANNER OF IDENTIFICATION OF GOODS.

(1) The buyer obtains a special property and an insurable interest in goods by identification of existing goods as goods to which the contract refers even though the goods so identified are non-conforming and he has an option to return or reject them. Such identification can be made at any time and in any manner explicitly agreed to by the parties. In the absence of explicit agreement identification occurs

(a) when the contract is made if it is for the sale of goods already existing and identified;

(b) if the contract is for the sale of future goods other than those described in paragraph (c), when goods are shipped, marked or otherwise designated by the seller as goods to which the contract refers;

(c) when the crops are planted or otherwise become growing crops or the young are conceived if the contract is for the sale of unborn young to be born within twelve months after contracting or for the sale of crops to be harvested within twelve months or the next normal harvest season after contracting whichever is longer.

(2) The seller retains an insurable interest in goods so long as title to or any security interest in the goods remains in him and where the identification is by the seller alone he may until default or insolvency or notification to the buyer that the identification is final substitute other goods for those identified.

(3) Nothing in this section impairs any insurable interest recognized under any other statute or rule of law.

§ 2-502. BUYER'S RIGHT TO GOODS ON SELLER'S INSOLVENCY.

(1) Subject to subsection (2) and even though the goods have not been shipped a buyer who has paid a part or all of the price of goods in which he has a special property under the provisions of the immediately preceding section may on making and keeping good a tender of any unpaid portion of their price recover them from the seller if the seller becomes insolvent within ten days after receipt of the first installment on their price.

(2) If the identification creating his special property has been made by the buyer he acquires the right to recover the goods only if they conform to the contract for sale.

§ 2-503. MANNER OF SELLER'S TENDER OF DELIVERY.

(1) Tender of delivery requires that the seller put and hold conforming goods at the buyer's disposition and give the buyer any notification reasonably necessary to enable him to take delivery. The manner, time and place for tender are determined by the agreement and this Article, and in particular

(a) tender must be at a reasonable hour, and if it is of goods they must be kept available for the period reasonably necessary to enable the buyer to take possession; but

(b) unless otherwise agreed the buyer must furnish facilities reasonably suited to the receipt of the goods.

(2) Where the case is within the next section respecting shipment tender requires that the seller comply with its provisions.

(3) Where the seller is required to deliver at a particular destination tender requires that he comply with subsection (1) and also in any appropriate case tender documents as described in subsections (4) and (5) of this section.

(4) Where goods are in the possession of a bailee and are to be delivered without being moved

(a) tender requires that the seller either tender a negotiable document of title covering such goods or procure acknowledgment by the bailee of the buyer's right to possession of the goods; but

(b) tender to the buyer of a non-negotiable document of title or of a written direction to the bailee to deliver is sufficient tender unless the buyer seasonably objects, and receipt by the bailee of notification of the buyer's rights fixes those rights as against the bailee and all third persons; but risk of loss of the goods and of any failure by the bailee to honor the non-negotiable document of title or to obey the direction remains on the seller until the buyer has had a reasonable time to present the document or direction, and a refusal by the bailee to honor the document or to obey the direction defeats the tender.

(5) Where the contract requires the seller to deliver documents

(a) he must tender all such documents in correct form, except as provided in this Article with respect to bills of lading in a set (subsection (2) of Section 2-323); and

(b) tender through customary banking channels is sufficient and dishonor of a draft accompanying the documents constitutes non-acceptance or rejection.

§ 2-504. SHIPMENT BY SELLER.

Where the seller is required or authorized to send the goods to the buyer and the contract does not require him to deliver them at a particular destination, then unless otherwise agreed he must

(a) put the goods in the possession of such a carrier and make such a contract for their transportation as may be reasonable having regard to the nature of the goods and other circumstances of the case; and

(b) obtain and promptly deliver or tender in due form any document necessary to enable the buyer to obtain possession of the goods or otherwise required by the agreement or by usage of trade; and

(c) promptly notify the buyer of the shipment.

Failure to notify the buyer under paragraph (c) or to make a proper contract under paragraph (a) is a ground for rejection only if material delay or loss ensues.

§ 2-505. SELLER'S SHIPMENT UNDER RESERVATION.

(1) Where the seller has identified goods to the contract by or before shipment:

(a) his procurement of a negotiable bill of lading to his own order or otherwise reserves in him a security interest in the goods. His procurement of the bill to the order of a financing agency or of the buyer indicates in addition only the seller's expectation of transferring that interest to the person named.

(b) a non-negotiable bill of lading to himself or his nominee reserves possession of the goods as security but except in a case of conditional delivery (subsection (2) of Section 2-507) a non-negotiable bill of lading naming the buyer as consignee reserves no security interest even though the seller retains possession of the bill of lading.

(2) When shipment by the seller with reservation of a security interest is in violation of the contract for sale it constitutes an improper contract for transportation within the preceding section but impairs neither the rights given to the buyer by shipment and identification of the goods to the contract nor the seller's powers as a holder of a negotiable document.

§ 2-506. RIGHTS OF FINANCING AGENCY.

(1) A financing agency by paying or purchasing for value a draft which relates to a shipment of goods acquires to the extent of the payment or

purchase and in addition to its own rights under the draft and any document of title securing it any rights of the shipper in the goods including the right to stop delivery and the shipper's right to have the draft honored by the buyer.

(2) The right to reimbursement of a financing agency which has in good faith honored or purchased the draft under commitment to or authority from the buyer is not impaired by subsequent discovery of defects with reference to any relevant document which was apparently regular on its face.

§ 2-507. EFFECT OF SELLER'S TENDER; DELIVERY ON CONDITION.

(1) Tender of delivery is a condition to the buyer's duty to accept the goods and, unless otherwise agreed, to his duty to pay for them. Tender entitles the seller to acceptance of the goods and to payment according to the contract.

(2) Where payment is due and demanded on the delivery to the buyer of goods or documents of title, his right as against the seller to retain or dispose of them is conditional upon his making the payment due.

§ 2-508. CURE BY SELLER OF IMPROPER TENDER OR DELIVERY; REPLACEMENT.

(1) Where any tender or delivery by the seller is rejected because non-conforming and the time for performance has not yet expired, the seller may seasonably notify the buyer of his intention to cure and may then within the contract time make a conforming delivery.

(2) Where the buyer rejects a non-conforming tender which the seller had reasonable grounds to believe would be acceptable with or without money allowance the seller may if he seasonably notifies the buyer have a further reasonable time to substitute a conforming tender.

§ 2-509. RISK OF LOSS IN THE ABSENCE OF BREACH.

(1) Where the contract requires or authorizes the seller to ship the goods by carrier

(a) if it does not require him to deliver them at a particular destination, the risk of loss passes to the buyer when the goods are duly delivered to the carrier even though the shipment is under reservation (Section 2-505); but

(b) if it does require him to deliver them at a particular destination and the goods are there duly tendered while in the possession of the carrier, the risk of loss passes to the buyer when the goods are there duly so tendered as to enable the buyer to take delivery.

(2) Where the goods are held by a bailee to be delivered without being moved, the risk of loss passes to the buyer

(a) on his receipt of a negotiable document of title covering the goods; or

(b) on acknowledgment by the bailee of the buyer's right to possession of the goods; or

(c) after his receipt of a non-negotiable document of title or other written direction to deliver, as provided in subsection (4)(b) of Section 2-503.

(3) In any case not within subsection (1) or (2), the risk of loss passes to the buyer on his receipt of the goods if the seller is a merchant; otherwise the risk passes to the buyer on tender of delivery.

(4) The provisions of this section are subject to contrary agreement of the parties and to the provisions of this Article on sale on approval (Section 2-327) and on effect of breach on risk of loss (Section 2-510).

§ 2-510. EFFECT OF BREACH ON RISK OF LOSS.

(1) Where a tender or delivery of goods so fails to conform to the contract as to give a right of rejection the risk of their loss remains on the seller until cure or acceptance.

(2) Where the buyer rightfully revokes acceptance he may to the extent of any deficiency in his effective insurance coverage treat the risk of loss as having rested on the seller from the beginning.

(3) Where the buyer as to conforming goods already identified to the contract for sale repudiates or is otherwise in breach before risk of their loss has passed to him, the seller may to the extent of any deficiency in his effective insurance coverage treat the risk of loss as resting on the buyer for a commercially reasonable time.

§ 2-511. TENDER OF PAYMENT BY BUYER; PAYMENT BY CHECK.

(1) Unless otherwise agreed tender of payment is a condition to the seller's duty to tender and complete any delivery.

(2) Tender of payment is sufficient when made by any means or in any manner current in the ordinary course of business unless the seller demands payment in legal tender and gives any extension of time reasonably necessary to procure it.

(3) Subject to the provisions of this Act on the effect of an instrument on an obligation (Section 3-310), payment by check is conditional and is defeated as between the parties by dishonor of the check on due presentment.

§ 2-512. PAYMENT BY BUYER BEFORE INSPECTION.

(1) Where the contract requires payment before inspection non-conformity of the goods does not excuse the buyer from so making payment unless

(a) the non-conformity appears without inspection; or

(b) despite tender of the required documents the circumstances would justify injunction against honor under the provisions of this Act (Section 5-114).

(2) Payment pursuant to subsection (1) does not constitute an acceptance of goods or impair the buyer's right to inspect or any of his remedies.

§ 2-513. BUYER'S RIGHT TO INSPECTION OF GOODS.

(1) Unless otherwise agreed and subject to subsection (3), where goods are tendered or delivered or identified to the contract for sale, the buyer has a right before payment or acceptance to inspect them at any reasonable place and time and in any reasonable manner. When the seller is required or authorized to send the goods to the buyer, the inspection may be after their arrival.

(2) Expenses of inspection must be borne by the buyer but may be recovered from the seller if the goods do not conform and are rejected.

(3) Unless otherwise agreed and subject to the provisions of this Article on C.I.F. contracts (subsection (3) of Section 2-321), the buyer is not entitled to inspect the goods before payment of the price when the contract provides

(a) for delivery "C.O.D." or on other like terms; or

(b) for payment against documents of title, except where such payment is due only after the goods are to become available for inspection.

(4) A place or method of inspection fixed by the parties is presumed to be exclusive but unless otherwise expressly agreed it does not postpone identification or shift the place for delivery or for passing the risk of loss. If compliance becomes impossible, inspection shall be as provided in this section unless the place or method fixed was clearly intended as an indispensable condition failure of which avoids the contract.

§ 2-514. WHEN DOCUMENTS DELIVERABLE ON ACCEPTANCE; WHEN ON PAYMENT.

Unless otherwise agreed documents against which a draft is drawn are to be delivered to the drawee on acceptance of the draft if it is payable more than three days after presentment; otherwise, only on payment.

§ 2-515. PRESERVING EVIDENCE OF GOODS IN DISPUTE.

In furtherance of the adjustment of any claim or dispute

(a) either party on reasonable notification to the other and for the purpose of ascertaining the facts and preserving evidence has the right to inspect, test and sample the goods including such of them as may be in the possession or control of the other; and

(b) the parties may agree to a third party inspection or survey to determine the conformity or condition of the goods and may agree that the findings shall be binding upon them in any subsequent litigation or adjustment.

§ 2-601. BUYER'S RIGHTS ON IMPROPER DELIVERY.

Subject to the provisions of this Article on breach in installment contracts (Section 2-612) and unless otherwise agreed under the sections on contractual limitations of remedy (Sections 2-718 and 2-719), if the goods or the tender of delivery fail in any respect to conform to the contract, the buyer may

(a) reject the whole; or

(b) accept the whole; or

(c) accept any commercial unit or units and reject the rest.

§ 2-602. MANNER AND EFFECT OF RIGHTFUL REJECTION.

(1) Rejection of goods must be within a reasonable time after their delivery or tender. It is ineffective unless the buyer seasonably notifies the seller.

(2) Subject to the provisions of the two following sections on rejected goods (Sections 2-603 and 2-604),

(a) after rejection any exercise of ownership by the buyer with respect to any commercial unit is wrongful as against the seller; and

(b) if the buyer has before rejection taken physical possession of goods in which he does not have a security interest under the provisions of this Article (subsection (3) of Section 2-711), he is under a duty after rejection to hold them with reasonable care at the seller's disposition for a time sufficient to permit the seller to remove them; but

(c) the buyer has no further obligations with regard to goods rightfully rejected.

(3) The seller's rights with respect to goods wrongfully rejected are governed by the provisions of this Article on Seller's remedies in general (Section 2-703).

§ 2-603. MERCHANT BUYER'S DUTIES AS TO RIGHTFULLY REJECTED GOODS.

(1) Subject to any security interest in the buyer (subsection (3) of Section 2-711), when the seller has no agent or place of business at the market of rejection a merchant buyer is under a duty after rejection of goods in his possession or control to follow any reasonable instructions received from the seller with respect to the goods and in the absence of such instructions to make reasonable efforts to sell them for the seller's account if they are perishable or threaten to decline in value speedily. Instructions are not reasonable if on demand indemnity for expenses is not forthcoming.

(2) When the buyer sells goods under subsection (1), he is entitled to reimbursement from the seller or out of the proceeds for reasonable expenses of caring for and selling them, and if the expenses include no selling commission then to such commission as is usual in the trade or if there is none to a reasonable sum not exceeding ten percent on the gross proceeds.

(3) In complying with this section the buyer is held only to good faith and good faith conduct hereunder is neither acceptance nor conversion nor the basis of an action for damages.

§ 2-604. BUYER'S OPTIONS AS TO SALVAGE OF RIGHTFULLY REJECTED GOODS.

Subject to the provisions of the immediately preceding section on perishables if the seller gives no instructions within a reasonable time after notification of rejection the buyer may store the rejected goods for the seller's account or reship them to him or resell them for the seller's account with reimbursement as provided in the preceding section. Such action is not acceptance or conversion.

§ 2-605. WAIVER OF BUYER'S OBJECTIONS BY FAILURE TO PARTICULARIZE.

(1) The buyer's failure to state in connection with rejection a particular defect which is ascertainable by reasonable inspection precludes him from relying on the unstated defect to justify rejection or to establish breach

(a) where the seller could have cured it if stated seasonably; or

(b) between merchants when the seller has after rejection made a request in writing for a full and final written statement of all defects on which the buyer proposes to rely.

(2) Payment against documents made without reservation of rights precludes recovery of the payment for defects apparent on the face of the documents.

§ 2-606. WHAT CONSTITUTES ACCEPTANCE OF GOODS.

(1) Acceptance of goods occurs when the buyer

(a) after a reasonable opportunity to inspect the goods signifies to the seller that the goods are conforming or that he will take or retain them in spite of their non-conformity; or

(b) fails to make an effective rejection (subsection (1) of Section 2-602), but such acceptance does not occur until the buyer has had a reasonable opportunity to inspect them; or

(c) does any act inconsistent with the seller's ownership; but if such act is wrongful as against the seller it is an acceptance only if ratified by him.

(2) Acceptance of a part of any commercial unit is acceptance of that entire unit.

§ 2-607. EFFECT OF ACCEPTANCE; NOTICE OF BREACH; BURDEN OF ESTABLISHING BREACH AFTER ACCEPTANCE; NOTICE OF CLAIM OR LITIGATION TO PERSON ANSWERABLE OVER.

(1) The buyer must pay at the contract rate for any goods accepted.

(2) Acceptance of goods by the buyer precludes rejection of the goods accepted and if made with knowledge of a non-conformity cannot be

revoked because of it unless the acceptance was on the reasonable assumption that the non-conformity would be seasonably cured but acceptance does not of itself impair any other remedy provided by this Article for non-conformity.

(3) Where a tender has been accepted

(a) the buyer must within a reasonable time after he discovers or should have discovered any breach notify the seller of breach or be barred from any remedy; and

(b) if the claim is one for infringement or the like (subsection (3) of Section 2-312) and the buyer is sued as a result of such a breach he must so notify the seller within a reasonable time after he receives notice of the litigation or be barred from any remedy over for liability established by the litigation.

(4) The burden is on the buyer to establish any breach with respect to the goods accepted.

(5) Where the buyer is sued for breach of a warranty or other obligation for which his seller is answerable over

(a) he may give his seller written notice of the litigation. If the notice states that the seller may come in and defend and that if the seller does not do so he will be bound in any action against him by his buyer by any determination of fact common to the two litigations, then unless the seller after seasonable receipt of the notice does come in and defend he is so bound.

(b) if the claim is one for infringement or the like (subsection (3) of Section 2-312) the original seller may demand in writing that his buyer turn over to him control of the litigation including settlement or else be barred from any remedy over and if he also agrees to bear all expense and to satisfy any adverse judgment, then unless the buyer after seasonable receipt of the demand does turn over control the buyer is so barred.

(6) The provisions of subsections (3), (4) and (5) apply to any obligation of a buyer to hold the seller harmless against infringement or the like (subsection (3) of Section 2-312).

§ 2-608. REVOCATION OF ACCEPTANCE IN WHOLE OR IN PART.

(1) The buyer may revoke his acceptance of a lot or commercial unit whose non-conformity substantially impairs its value to him if he has accepted it

(a) on the reasonable assumption that its non-conformity would be cured and it has not been seasonably cured; or

(b) without discovery of such non-conformity if his acceptance was reasonably induced either by the difficulty of discovery before acceptance or by the seller's assurances.

(2) Revocation of acceptance must occur within a reasonable time after the buyer discovers or should have discovered the ground for it and

before any substantial change in condition of the goods which is not caused by their own defects. It is not effective until the buyer notifies the seller of it.

(3) A buyer who so revokes has the same rights and duties with regard to the goods involved as if he had rejected them.

§ 2-609. RIGHT TO ADEQUATE ASSURANCE OF PERFORMANCE.

(1) A contract for sale imposes an obligation on each party that the other's expectation of receiving due performance will not be impaired. When reasonable grounds for insecurity arise with respect to the performance of either party the other may in writing demand adequate assurance of due performance and until he receives such assurance may if commercially reasonable suspend any performance for which he has not already received the agreed return.

(2) Between merchants the reasonableness of grounds for insecurity and the adequacy of any assurance offered shall be determined according to commercial standards.

(3) Acceptance of any improper delivery or payment does not prejudice the aggrieved party's right to demand adequate assurance of future performance.

(4) After receipt of a justified demand failure to provide within a reasonable time not exceeding thirty days such assurance of due performance as is adequate under the circumstances of the particular case is a repudiation of the contract.

§ 2-610. ANTICIPATORY REPUDIATION.

When either party repudiates the contract with respect to a performance not yet due the loss of which will substantially impair the value of the contract to the other, the aggrieved party may

(a) for a commercially reasonable time await performance by the repudiating party; or

(b) resort to any remedy for breach (Section 2-703 or Section 2-711), even though he has notified the repudiating party that he would await the latter's performance and has urged retraction; and

(c) in either case suspend his own performance or proceed in accordance with the provisions of this Article on the seller's right to identify goods to the contract notwithstanding breach or to salvage unfinished goods (Section 2-704).

§ 2-611. RETRACTION OF ANTICIPATORY REPUDIATION.

(1) Until the repudiating party's next performance is due he can retract his repudiation unless the aggrieved party has since the repudiation cancelled or materially changed his position or otherwise indicated that he considers the repudiation final.

(2) Retraction may be by any method which clearly indicates to the aggrieved party that the repudiating party intends to perform, but must include any assurance justifiably demanded under the provisions of this Article (Section 2-609).

(3) Retraction reinstates the repudiating party's rights under the contract with due excuse and allowance to the aggrieved party for any delay occasioned by the repudiation.

§ 2-612. "INSTALLMENT CONTRACT"; BREACH.

(1) An "installment contract" is one which requires or authorizes the delivery of goods in separate lots to be separately accepted, even though the contract contains a clause "each delivery is a separate contract" or its equivalent.

(2) The buyer may reject any installment which is non-conforming if the non-conformity substantially impairs the value of that installment and cannot be cured or if the non-conformity is a defect in the required documents; but if the non-conformity does not fall within subsection (3) and the seller gives adequate assurance of its cure the buyer must accept that installment.

(3) Whenever non-conformity or default with respect to one or more installments substantially impairs the value of the whole contract there is a breach of the whole. But the aggrieved party reinstates the contract if he accepts a non-conforming installment without seasonably notifying of cancellation or if he brings an action with respect only to past installments or demands performance as to future installments.

§ 2-613. CASUALTY TO IDENTIFIED GOODS.

Where the contract requires for its performance goods identified when the contract is made, and the goods suffer casualty without fault of either party before the risk of loss passes to the buyer, or in a proper case under a "no arrival, no sale" term (Section 2-324) then

(a) if the loss is total the contract is avoided; and

(b) if the loss is partial or the goods have so deteriorated as no longer to conform to the contract the buyer may nevertheless demand inspection and at his option either treat the contract as avoided or accept the goods with due allowance from the contract price for the deterioration or the deficiency in quantity but without further right against the seller.

§ 2-614. SUBSTITUTED PERFORMANCE.

(1) Where without fault of either party the agreed berthing, loading, or unloading facilities fail or an agreed type of carrier becomes unavailable or the agreed manner of delivery otherwise becomes commercially impracticable but a commercially reasonable substitute is available, such substitute performance must be tendered and accepted.

(2) If the agreed means or manner of payment fails because of domestic or foreign governmental regulation, the seller may withhold or stop delivery unless the buyer provides a means or manner of payment which is commercially a substantial equivalent. If delivery has already been taken, payment by the means or in the manner provided by the regulation discharges the buyer's obligation unless the regulation is discriminatory, oppressive or predatory.

§ 2-615. EXCUSE BY FAILURE OF PRESUPPOSED CONDITIONS.

Except so far as a seller may have assumed a greater obligation and subject to the preceding section on substituted performance:

(a) Delay in delivery or non-delivery in whole or in part by a seller who complies with paragraphs (b) and (c) is not a breach of his duty under a contract for sale if performance as agreed has been made impracticable by the occurrence of a contingency the non-occurrence of which was a basic assumption on which the contract was made or by compliance in good faith with any applicable foreign or domestic governmental regulation or order whether or not it later proves to be invalid.

(b) Where the causes mentioned in paragraph (a) affect only a part of the seller's capacity to perform, he must allocate production and deliveries among his customers but may at his option include regular customers not then under contract as well as his own requirements for further manufacture. He may so allocate in any manner which is fair and reasonable.

(c) The seller must notify the buyer seasonably that there will be delay or non-delivery and, when allocation is required under paragraph (b), of the estimated quota thus made available for the buyer.

§ 2-616. PROCEDURE ON NOTICE CLAIMING EXCUSE.

(1) Where the buyer receives notification of a material or indefinite delay or an allocation justified under the preceding section he may by written notification to the seller as to any delivery concerned, and where the prospective deficiency substantially impairs the value of the whole contract under the provisions of this Article relating to breach of installment contracts (Section 2-612), then also as to the whole,

(a) terminate and thereby discharge any unexecuted portion of the contract; or

(b) modify the contract by agreeing to take his available quota in substitution.

(2) If after receipt of such notification from the seller the buyer fails so to modify the contract within a reasonable time not exceeding thirty days the contract lapses with respect to any deliveries affected.

(3) The provisions of this section may not be negated by agreement except in so far as the seller has assumed a greater obligation under the preceding section.

§ 2-701. REMEDIES FOR BREACH OF COLLATERAL CONTRACTS NOT IMPAIRED.

Remedies for breach of any obligation or promise collateral or ancillary to a contract for sale are not impaired by the provisions of this Article.

§ 2-702. SELLER'S REMEDIES ON DISCOVERY OF BUYER'S INSOLVENCY.

(1) Where the seller discovers the buyer to be insolvent he may refuse delivery except for cash including payment for all goods theretofore delivered under the contract, and stop delivery under this Article (Section 2-705).

(2) Where the seller discovers that the buyer has received goods on credit while insolvent he may reclaim the goods upon demand made within ten days after the receipt, but if misrepresentation of solvency has been made to the particular seller in writing within three months before delivery the ten day limitation does not apply. Except as provided in this subsection the seller may not base a right to reclaim goods on the buyer's fraudulent or innocent misrepresentation of solvency or of intent to pay.

(3) The seller's right to reclaim under subsection (2) is subject to the rights of a buyer in ordinary course or other good faith purchaser under this Article (Section 2-403). Successful reclamation of goods excludes all other remedies with respect to them.

§ 2-703. SELLER'S REMEDIES IN GENERAL.

Where the buyer wrongfully rejects or revokes acceptance of goods or fails to make a payment due on or before delivery or repudiates with respect to a part or the whole, then with respect to any goods directly affected and, if the breach is of the whole contract (Section 2-612), then also with respect to the whole undelivered balance, the aggrieved seller may
(a) withhold delivery of such goods;
(b) stop delivery by any bailee as hereafter provided (Section 2-705);
(c) proceed under the next section respecting goods still unidentified to the contract;
(d) resell and recover damages as hereafter provided (Section 2-706);
(e) recover damages for non-acceptance (Section 2-708) or in a proper case the price (Section 2-709);
(f) cancel.

§ 2-704. SELLER'S RIGHT TO IDENTIFY GOODS TO THE CONTRACT NOTWITHSTANDING BREACH OR TO SALVAGE UNFINISHED GOODS.

(1) An aggrieved seller under the preceding section may
(a) identify to the contract conforming goods not already identified if at the time he learned of the breach they are in his possession or control;
(b) treat as the subject of resale goods which have demonstrably been intended for the particular contract even though those goods are unfinished.

(2) Where the goods are unfinished an aggrieved seller may in the exercise of reasonable commercial judgment for the purposes of avoiding loss and of effective realization either complete the manufacture and wholly identify the goods to the contract or cease manufacture and resell for scrap or salvage value or proceed in any other reasonable manner.

§ 2-705. SELLER'S STOPPAGE OF DELIVERY IN TRANSIT OR OTHERWISE.

(1) The seller may stop delivery of goods in the possession of a carrier or other bailee when he discovers the buyer to be insolvent (Section 2-702) and may stop delivery of carload, truckload, planeload or larger shipments of express or freight when the buyer repudiates or fails to make a payment due before delivery or if for any other reason the seller has a right to withhold or reclaim the goods.

(2) As against such buyer the seller may stop delivery until

(a) receipt of the goods by the buyer; or

(b) acknowledgment to the buyer by any bailee of the goods except a carrier that the bailee holds the goods for the buyer; or

(c) such acknowledgment to the buyer by a carrier by reshipment or as warehouseman; or

(d) negotiation to the buyer of any negotiable document of title covering the goods.

(3) (a) To stop delivery the seller must so notify as to enable the bailee by reasonable diligence to prevent delivery of the goods.

(b) After such notification the bailee must hold and deliver the goods according to the directions of the seller but the seller is liable to the bailee for any ensuing charges or damages.

(c) If a negotiable document of title has been issued for goods the bailee is not obliged to obey a notification to stop until surrender of the document.

(d) A carrier who has issued a non-negotiable bill of lading is not obliged to obey a notification to stop received from a person other than the consignor.

§ 2-706. SELLER'S RESALE INCLUDING CONTRACT FOR RESALE.

(1) Under the conditions stated in Section 2-703 on seller's remedies, the seller may resell the goods concerned or the undelivered balance thereof. Where the resale is made in good faith and in a commercially reasonable manner the seller may recover the difference between the resale price and the contract price together with any incidental damages allowed under the provisions of this Article (Section 2-710), but less expenses saved in consequence of the buyer's breach.

(2) Except as otherwise provided in subsection (3) or unless otherwise agreed resale may be at public or private sale including sale by way of

one or more contracts to sell or of identification to an existing contract of the seller. Sale may be as a unit or in parcels and at any time and place and on any terms but every aspect of the sale including the method, manner, time, place and terms must be commercially reasonable. The resale must be reasonably identified as referring to the broken contract, but it is not necessary that the goods be in existence or that any or all of them have been identified to the contract before the breach.

(3) Where the resale is at private sale the seller must give the buyer reasonable notification of his intention to resell.

(4) Where the resale is at public sale

(a) only identified goods can be sold except where there is a recognized market for a public sale of futures in goods of the kind; and

(b) it must be made at a usual place or market for public sale if one is reasonably available and except in the case of goods which are perishable or threaten to decline in value speedily the seller must give the buyer reasonable notice of the time and place of the resale; and

(c) if the goods are not to be within the view of those attending the sale the notification of sale must state the place where the goods are located and provide for their reasonable inspection by prospective bidders; and

(d) the seller may buy.

(5) A purchaser who buys in good faith at a resale takes the goods free of any rights of the original buyer even though the seller fails to comply with one or more of the requirements of this section.

(6) The seller is not accountable to the buyer for any profit made on any resale. A person in the position of a seller (Section 2-707) or a buyer who has rightfully rejected or justifiably revoked acceptance must account for any excess over the amount of his security interest, as hereinafter defined (subsection (3) of Section 2-711).

§ 2-707. "PERSON IN THE POSITION OF A SELLER".

(1) A "person in the position of a seller" includes as against a principal an agent who has paid or become responsible for the price of goods on behalf of his principal or anyone who otherwise holds a security interest or other right in goods similar to that of a seller.

(2) A person in the position of a seller may as provided in this Article withhold or stop delivery (Section 2-705) and resell (Section 2-706) and recover incidental damages (Section 2-710).

§ 2-708. SELLER'S DAMAGES FOR NON-ACCEPTANCE OR REPUDIATION.

(1) Subject to subsection (2) and to the provisions of this Article with respect to proof of market price (Section 2-723), the measure of damages for non-acceptance or repudiation by the buyer is the difference between the market price at the time and place for tender and the unpaid contract price together with any incidental damages provided in this Article

(Section 2-710), but less expenses saved in consequence of the buyer's breach.

(2) If the measure of damages provided in subsection (1) is inadequate to put the seller in as good a position as performance would have done then the measure of damages is the profit (including reasonable overhead) which the seller would have made from full performance by the buyer, together with any incidental damages provided in this Article (Section 2-710), due allowance for costs reasonably incurred and due credit for payments or proceeds of resale.

§ 2-709. ACTION FOR THE PRICE.

(1) When the buyer fails to pay the price as it becomes due the seller may recover, together with any incidental damages under the next section, the price

(a) of goods accepted or of conforming goods lost or damaged within a commercially reasonable time after risk of their loss has passed to the buyer; and

(b) of goods identified to the contract if the seller is unable after reasonable effort to resell them at a reasonable price or the circumstances reasonably indicate that such effort will be unavailing.

(2) Where the seller sues for the price he must hold for the buyer any goods which have been identified to the contract and are still in his control except that if resale becomes possible he may resell them at any time prior to the collection of the judgment. The net proceeds of any such resale must be credited to the buyer and payment of the judgment entitles him to any goods not resold.

(3) After the buyer has wrongfully rejected or revoked acceptance of the goods or has failed to make a payment due or has repudiated (Section 2-610), a seller who is held not entitled to the price under this section shall nevertheless be awarded damages for non-acceptance under the preceding section.

§ 2-710. SELLER'S INCIDENTAL DAMAGES.

Incidental damages to an aggrieved seller include any commercially reasonable charges, expenses or commissions incurred in stopping delivery, in the transportation, care and custody of goods after the buyer's breach, in connection with return or resale of the goods or otherwise resulting from the breach.

§ 2-711. BUYER'S REMEDIES IN GENERAL; BUYER'S SECURITY INTEREST IN REJECTED GOODS.

(1) Where the seller fails to make delivery or repudiates or the buyer rightfully rejects or justifiably revokes acceptance then with respect to any goods involved, and with respect to the whole if the breach goes to

the whole contract (Section 2-612), the buyer may cancel and whether or not he has done so may in addition to recovering so much of the price as has been paid

(a) "cover" and have damages under the next section as to all the goods affected whether or not they have been identified to the contract; or

(b) recover damages for non-delivery as provided in this Article (Section 2-713).

(2) Where the seller fails to deliver or repudiates the buyer may also

(a) if the goods have been identified recover them as provided in this Article (Section 2-502); or

(b) in a proper case obtain specific performance or replevy the goods as provided in this Article (Section 2-716).

(3) On rightful rejection or justifiable revocation of acceptance a buyer has a security interest in goods in his possession or control for any payments made on their price and any expenses reasonably incurred in their inspection, receipt, transportation, care and custody and may hold such goods and resell them in like manner as an aggrieved seller (Section 2-706).

§ 2-712. "COVER"; BUYER'S PROCUREMENT OF SUBSTITUTE GOODS.

(1) After a breach within the preceding section the buyer may "cover" by making in good faith and without unreasonable delay any reasonable purchase of or contract to purchase goods in substitution for those due from the seller.

(2) The buyer may recover from the seller as damages the difference between the cost of cover and the contract price together with any incidental or consequential damages as hereinafter defined (Section 2-715), but less expenses saved in consequence of the seller's breach.

(3) Failure of the buyer to effect cover within this Section does not bar him from any other remedy.

§ 2-713. BUYER'S DAMAGES FOR NON-DELIVERY OR REPUDIATION.

(1) Subject to the provisions of this Article with respect to proof of market price (Section 2-723), the measure of damages for non-delivery or repudiation by the seller is the difference between the market price at the time when the buyer learned of the breach and the contract price together with any incidental and consequential damages provided in this Article (Section 2-715), but less expenses saved in consequence of the seller's breach.

(2) Market price is to be determined as of the place for tender or, in cases of rejection after arrival or revocation of acceptance, as of the place of arrival.

§ 2-714. BUYER'S DAMAGES FOR BREACH IN REGARD TO ACCEPTED GOODS.

(1) Where the buyer has accepted goods and given notification (subsection (3) of Section 2-607) he may recover as damages for any nonconformity of tender the loss resulting in the ordinary course of events from the seller's breach as determined in any manner which is reasonable.

(2) The measure of damages for breach of warranty is the difference at the time and place of acceptance between the value of the goods accepted and the value they would have had if they had been as warranted, unless special circumstances show proximate damages of a different amount.

(3) In a proper case any incidental and consequential damages under the next section may also be recovered.

§ 2-715. BUYER'S INCIDENTAL AND CONSEQUENTIAL DAMAGES.

(1) Incidental damages resulting from the seller's breach include expenses reasonably incurred in inspection, receipt, transportation and care and custody of goods rightfully rejected, any commercially reasonable charges, expenses or commissions in connection with effecting cover and any other reasonable expense incident to the delay or other breach.

(2) Consequential damages resulting from the seller's breach include

(a) any loss resulting from general or particular requirements and needs of which the seller at the time of contracting had reason to know and which could not reasonably be prevented by cover or otherwise; and

(b) injury to person or property proximately resulting from any breach of warranty.

§ 2-716. BUYER'S RIGHT TO SPECIFIC PERFORMANCE OR REPLEVIN.

(1) Specific performance may be decreed where the goods are unique or in other proper circumstances.

(2) The decree for specific performance may include such terms and conditions as to payment of the price, damages, or other relief as the court may deem just.

(3) The buyer has a right of replevin for goods identified to the contract if after reasonable effort he is unable to effect cover for such goods or the circumstances reasonably indicate that such effort will be unavailing or if the goods have been shipped under reservation and satisfaction of the security interest in them has been made or tendered.

§ 2-717. DEDUCTION OF DAMAGES FROM THE PRICE.

The buyer on notifying the seller of his intention to do so may deduct all or any part of the damages resulting from any breach of the contract from any part of the price still due under the same contract.

§ 2-718. LIQUIDATION OR LIMITATION OF DAMAGES, DEPOSITS.

(1) Damages for breach by either party may be liquidated in the agreement but only at an amount which is reasonable in the light of the anticipated or actual harm caused by the breach, the difficulties of proof of loss, and the inconvenience or nonfeasibility of otherwise obtaining an adequate remedy. A term fixing unreasonably large liquidated damages is void as a penalty.

(2) Where the seller justifiably withholds delivery of goods because of the buyer's breach, the buyer is entitled to restitution of any amount by which the sum of his payments exceeds

(a) the amount to which the seller is entitled by virtue of terms liquidating the seller's damages in accordance with subsection (1), or

(b) in the absence of such terms, twenty percent of the value of the total performance for which the buyer is obligated under the contract or $500, whichever is smaller.

(3) The buyer's right to restitution under subsection (2) is subject to offset to the extent that the seller establishes

(a) a right to recover damages under the provisions of this Article other than subsection (1), and

(b) the amount or value of any benefits received by the buyer directly or indirectly by reason of the contract.

(4) Where a seller has received payment in goods their reasonable value or the proceeds of their resale shall be treated as payments for the purposes of subsection (2); but if the seller has notice of the buyer's breach before reselling goods received in part performance, his resale is subject to the conditions laid down in this Article on resale by an aggrieved seller (Section 2-706).

§ 2-719. CONTRACTUAL MODIFICATION OR LIMITATION OF REMEDY.

(1) Subject to the provisions of subsections (2) and (3) of this section and of the preceding section on liquidation and limitation of damages,

(a) the agreement may provide for remedies in addition to or in substitution for those provided in this Article and may limit or alter the measure of damages recoverable under this Article, as by limiting the buyer's remedies to return of the goods and repayment of the price or to repair and replacement of non-conforming goods or parts; and

(b) resort to a remedy as provided is optional unless the remedy is expressly agreed to be exclusive, in which case it is the sole remedy.

(2) Where circumstances cause an exclusive or limited remedy to fail of its essential purpose, remedy may be had as provided in this Act.

(3) Consequential damages may be limited or excluded unless the limitation or exclusion is unconscionable. Limitation of consequential damages for injury to the person in the case of consumer goods is prima

facie unconscionable but limitation of damages where the loss is commercial is not.

§ 2-720. EFFECT OF "CANCELLATION" OF "RESCISSION" ON CLAIMS FOR ANTECEDENT BREACH.

Unless the contrary intention clearly appears, expressions of "cancellation" or "rescission" of the contract or the like shall not be construed as a renunciation or discharge of any claim in damages for an antecedent breach.

§ 2-721. REMEDIES FOR FRAUD.

Remedies for material misrepresentation or fraud include all remedies available under this Article for non-fraudulent breach. Neither rescission or a claim for rescission of the contract for sale nor rejection or return of the goods shall bar or be deemed inconsistent with a claim for damages or other remedy.

§ 2-722. WHO CAN SUE THIRD PARTIES FOR INJURY TO GOODS.

Where a third party so deals with goods which have been identified to a contract for sale as to cause actionable injury to a party to that contract

(a) a right of action against the third party is in either party to the contract for sale who has title to or a security interest or a special property or an insurable interest in the goods; and if the goods have been destroyed or converted a right of action is also in the party who either bore the risk of loss under the contract for sale or has since the injury assumed that risk as against the other;

(b) if at the time of the injury the party plaintiff did not bear the risk of loss as against the other party to the contract for sale and there is no arrangement between them for disposition of the recovery, his suit or settlement is, subject to his own interest, as a fiduciary for the other party to the contract;

(c) either party may with the consent of the other sue for the benefit of whom it may concern.

§ 2-723. PROOF OF MARKET PRICE; TIME AND PLACE.

(1) If an action based on anticipatory repudiation comes to trial before the time for performance with respect to some or all of the goods, any damages based on market price (Section 2-708 or Section 2-713) shall be determined according to the price of such goods prevailing at the time when the aggrieved party learned of the repudiation.

(2) If evidence of a price prevailing at the times or places described in this Article is not readily available the price prevailing within any reasonable time before or after the time described or at any other place

which in commercial judgment or under usage of trade would serve as a reasonable substitute for the one described may be used, making any proper allowance for the cost of transporting the goods to or from such other place.

(3) Evidence of a relevant price prevailing at a time or place other than the one described in this Article offered by one party is not admissible unless and until he has given the other party such notice as the court finds sufficient to prevent unfair surprise.

§ 2-724. ADMISSIBILITY OF MARKET QUOTATIONS.

Whenever the prevailing price or value of any goods regularly bought and sold in any established commodity market is in issue, reports in official publications or trade journals or in newspapers or periodicals of general circulation published as the reports of such market shall be admissible in evidence. The circumstances of the preparation of such a report may be shown to affect its weight but not its admissibility.

§ 2-725. STATUTE OF LIMITATIONS IN CONTRACTS FOR SALE.

(1) An action for breach of any contract for sale must be commenced within four years after the cause of action has accrued. By the original agreement the parties may reduce the period of limitation to not less than one year but may not extend it.

(2) A cause of action accrues when the breach occurs, regardless of the aggrieved party's lack of knowledge of the breach. A breach of warranty occurs when tender of delivery is made, except that where a warranty explicitly extends to future performance of the goods and discovery of the breach must await the time of such performance the cause of action accrues when the breach is or should have been discovered.

(3) Where an action commenced within the time limited by subsection (1) is so terminated as to leave available a remedy by another action for the same breach such other action may be commenced after the expiration of the time limited and within six months after the termination of the first action unless the termination resulted from voluntary discontinuance or from dismissal for failure or neglect to prosecute.

(4) This section does not alter the law on tolling of the statute of limitations nor does it apply to causes of action which have accrued before this Act becomes effective.

APPENDIX B

Glossary

APPENDIX B: GLOSSARY

All Entries Are Excerpted from *Black's Law Dictionary,* Sixth Edition (1996).

A

Acceptance   Compliance by offeree with terms and conditions of offer constitute an "acceptance." The offeree's notification or expression to the offeror that he or she agrees to be bound by the terms of the offeror's proposal. UCC § 2-606 provides three ways a buyer can accept goods: (1) by signifying to the seller that the goods are conforming or that he will accept them in spite of their nonconformity, (2) by failing to make an effective rejection, and (3) by doing an act inconsistent with the seller's ownership.

Accord and Satisfaction   A method of discharging a claim whereby the parties agree to give and accept something in settlement of the claim and perform the agreement, the "accord" being the agreement and the "satisfaction" its execution or performance. It is a new contract substituted for an old contract which is thereby discharged, or for an obligation or cause of action which is settled, and must have all of the elements of a valid contract.

Ambiguity   Language in contract is "ambiguous" when it is reasonably capable of being understood in more than one sense. Test for determining whether a contract is "ambiguous" is whether reasonable persons would find the contract subject to more than one interpretation.

Anticipatory [Repudiation or] Breach of Contract   The assertion by a party to a contract that he will not perform a future obligation as required by the contract. Such occurs when a party to an executory contract manifests a definite and unequivocal intent prior to time fixed in contract that it will not render its performance under the contract when that time arrives. In such a case, the other party may treat the contract as ended.

Assignment   A transfer or making over to another of the whole of any property, real or personal, in possession or in action, or of any estate or right therein [including a contract].

B

Bilateral Contract   [A] contract in which both the contracting parties are bound to fulfill obligations reciprocally toward each other, as in a contract of sale, when one becomes bound to deliver the thing sold, and the other to pay the price of it. A contract executory on both sides, and one which includes both rights and duties on each side. Contract formed by the exchange of promises in which the promise of one party is consideration supporting the promise of the other.

C

Capacity Legal qualification (i.e., legal age), competency, power, or fitness. Mental ability to understand the nature and effects of one's acts. Capacity to sue. The legal ability of a particular individual or entity to sue in, or to be brought into, the courts of a forum.

Compensatory Damages Compensatory [or expectation or expectancy] damages are such as will compensate the injured party for the injury sustained, and nothing more; such as will simply make good or replace the loss caused by the wrong or injury. Damages awarded to a person as compensation, indemnity, or restitution for harm sustained by him. The rationale behind compensatory damages is to restore the injured party to the position she was in prior to the injury.

Concurrent Conditions Those which are mutually dependent and are to be performed at the same time or simultaneously.

Condition A clause in a contract or agreement which has for its object to suspend, rescind, or modify the principal obligation. A qualification, restriction, or limitation modifying or destroying the original act with which it is connected; an event, fact, or the like that is necessary to the occurrence of some other, though not its cause; a prerequisite; a stipulation.

Condition Precedent [O]ne that is to be performed before the agreement becomes effective, and which calls for the happening of some event or the performance of some act after the terms of the contract have been agreed on, before the contract shall be binding on the parties; e.g., under disability insurance contract, insured is required to submit proof of disability before insurer is required to pay.

Condition Subsequent [A]ny condition which divests liability which has already attached on the failure to fulfill the condition as applied in contracts, a provision giving one party the right to divest himself of liability and obligation to perform further if the other party fails to meet condition, e.g., submit dispute to arbitration.

Consequential Damages Such damage, loss, or injury as does not flow directly and immediately from the act of the party, but only from some of the consequences or results of such act. Consequential damages resulting from a seller's breach of contract include any loss resulting from general or particular requirements and needs of which the seller at the time of contracting had reason to know and which could not reasonably be prevented (UCC § 2-715(2)).

Consideration   The inducement to a contract. The cause, motive, price, or impelling influence which induces a contracting party to enter into a contract. The reason or material cause of a contract. Some right, interest, profit, or benefit accruing to one party, or some forbearance, detriment, loss, or responsibility, given, suffered, or undertaken by the other.

Contract   An agreement between two or more persons which creates an obligation to do or not to do a particular thing. As defined in Restatement, Second, Contracts § 3: "A contract is a promise or a set of promises for the breach of which the law gives a remedy, or the performance of which the law in some way recognizes as a duty." A legal relationship consisting of the rights and duties of the contracting parties; a promise or set of promises constituting an agreement between the parties that gives each a legal duty to the other and also the right to seek a remedy for the breach of those duties. Its essentials are competent parties, subject matter, a legal consideration, mutuality of agreement, and mutuality of obligation.

Course of Dealing   A sequence of previous acts and conduct between the parties to a particular transaction which is fairly to be regarded as establishing a common basis of understanding for interpreting their expressions and other conduct (UCC § 1-205(1)).

Course of Performance   The understandings of performance which develop by conduct without objection between two parties during the performance of an executory contract.

Cover   The right of a buyer, after breach by a seller, to purchase goods in the open market in substitution for those due from the seller, if such purchase is made in good faith and without unreasonable delay. The buyer may then recover as damages the difference between the cost of cover and the contract price, plus any incidental and consequential damages but less expenses saved in consequence of the seller's breach (UCC § 2-712(1) and (2)).

Creditor Beneficiary   A third person to whom performance of promise comes in satisfaction of legal duty. A creditor who has rights in a contract made by the debtor and a third person, when the terms of the contract obligate the third person to pay the debt owed to the creditor. The creditor beneficiary can enforce the debt against either party.

D

Delegation   The change of one debtor for another, when he who is indebted substitutes a third person who obligates himself in his stead, [though] the creditor retains his rights against the original debtor.

Discharge   In contract law, discharge occurs either when the parties have performed their obligations in the contract, or when events, the conduct of the parties, or the operation of law releases the parties from performing.

Divisible Contract   When a contract consists of many parts, which may be considered as parts of one whole, the contract is entire. When the parts may be considered as so many distinct contracts, entered into at one time, and expressed in the same instrument, but not thereby made one contract, the contract is a separable [or divisible] contract. But, if the consideration of the contract is single and entire, the contract must be held to be entire, although the subject of the contract may consist of several distinct and wholly independent items.

Donee Beneficiary   A person not a party to a contract but to whom the benefits of a contract flow as a direct result of an intention to make a gift to that person. In a third-party contract, the person who takes the benefit of the contract though there is no privity between him and the contracting parties.

E

Expectancy or Expectation Damages   As awarded in actions for nonperformance of contract, such damages are calculable by subtracting the injured party's actual dollar position as a result of the breach from that party's projected dollar position had performance occurred. The goal is to ascertain the dollar amount necessary to ensure that the aggrieved party's position after the award will be the same, to the extent money can achieve the goal, as if the other party had performed.

Express Contract   An express contract is an actual agreement of the parties, the terms of which are openly uttered or declared at the time of making it, being stated in distinct and explicit language, either orally or in writing.

F

Firm Offer   As defined by UCC, an offer by a merchant to buy or sell goods in a signed writing which by its terms give assurance that it will be held open. Such is not revocable for lack of consideration during the time stated or if no time is stated for a reasonable time, but in no event may such period of irrevocability exceed three months; but any such term of assurance on a form supplied by the offeree must be separately signed by the offeror (UCC § 2-205).

Foreseeability (Foreseeable)   The ability to see or know in advance; e.g., the reasonable anticipation that harm or injury is a likely result from certain acts or omissions. That which is objectively reasonable to expect, not merely what might conceivably occur.

Fraud in Factum   Misrepresentation as to the nature of a writing that a person signs with neither knowledge nor reasonable opportunity to obtain knowledge of its character or essential terms.

Fraud in Inducement   Fraud connected with underlying transaction and not with the nature of the contract or document signed. Misrepresentation as to the terms, quality or other aspects of a contractual relation, venture or other transaction that leads a person to agree to enter into the transaction with a false impression or understanding of the risks, duties, or obligations she has undertaken.

Frustration   This doctrine provides, generally, that when existence of a specific thing is, either by terms of contract or in contemplation of parties, necessary for performance of a promise in the contract, duty to perform promise is discharged if thing is no longer in existence at time for performance.

I

Implied Contract   An implied contract is one not created or evidenced by the explicit agreement of the parties, but inferred by the law, as a matter of reason and justice from their acts or conduct, the circumstances surrounding the transaction making it a reasonable, or even a necessary, assumption that a contract existed between them by tacit understanding.

Impossibility   A doctrine under which a party to a contract is relieved of his duty to perform when performance has become impossible or totally impracticable (through no fault of the party). As a defense to nonperformance, such arises when performance is not possible because of, for example, destruction of subject of contract or death of person necessary for performance or where act contracted for has become illegal . . . [and] one basic part of the doctrine is that the impossibility of performance must be objective rather than merely subjective.

Impracticability   A broadened interpretation of the doctrine of impossibility which holds that a party to a contract for the sale of goods will be relieved of his or her duty to perform when the premise (e.g., existence of certain goods) on which the contract was based no longer exists due to unforeseeable events (UCC § 2-615).

Incapacity   Want of legal, physical, or intellectual capacity; want of power or ability to take or dispose; want of legal ability to act. Inefficiency; incompetency; lack of adequate power.

Incidental Beneficiary   Since there will often be many people indirectly or even directly benefited by any given contractual performance, the term "incidental beneficiary" is used to describe those persons who would benefit by the performance but who were not intended by the parties to be benefited and who thus cannot enforce the contract.

L

Liquidated Damages   Liquidated damages are the sum which a party to a contract agrees to pay if he breaks some promise and, which having been arrived at by good faith effort to estimate actual damage that will probably ensue from breach, is recoverable as agreed damages if breach occurs. Such are those damages which are reasonably ascertainable at time of breach, measurable by fixed or established external standard, or by standard apparent from documents upon which plaintiffs based their claim.

M

Mailbox Rule   In contract law, unless otherwise agreed or provided by law, acceptance of offer is effective when deposited in mail if properly addressed.

Material   Important; more or less necessary; having influence or effect; going to the merits; having to do with matter, as distinguished from form. Representation relating to matter which is so substantial and important as to influence party to whom made is "material."

Mental Capacity   The ability to understand the nature and effect of the act in which a person is engaged and the business he or she is transacting. Such a measure of intelligence, understanding, memory, and judgment relative to the particular transaction (e.g., making of will or entering into contract) as will enable the person to understand the nature, terms, and effect of her act.

Misrepresentation   [A]n intentional false statement respecting a matter of fact, made by one of the parties to a contract, which is material to the contract and influential in producing it. A "misrepresentation" which justifies the rescission of a contract is a false statement of a substantive fact, or any conduct which leads to a belief of a substantive fact material to proper understanding of the matter in hand, made with intent to deceive or mislead.

Mitigation of Damages   Doctrine of "mitigation of damages" (sometimes called doctrine of avoidable consequences) imposes on party injured by breach of contract or tort duty to exercise reasonable diligence and ordinary care in attempting to minimize his damages, or avoid aggravating the injury, after breach or injury has been inflicted and care and diligence required of him is the same as that which would be used by a man of ordinary prudence under like circumstances.

Mutual Mistake   Mutual mistake with regard to a contract, justifying reformation, exists when there has been a meeting of the minds of the parties and an agreement actually entered into but the agreement in its written form does not express what was really intended by the parties.

N

Novation   A type of substituted contract that has the effect of adding a party, either as obligor or obligee, who was not a party to the original duty. Substitution of a new contract, debt, or obligation for an existing one, between the same or different parties. The requisites of a novation are a previous valid obligation, an agreement of all the parties to a new contract, the extinguishment of the old obligation, and the validity of the new one.

O

Offer   A proposal to do a thing or pay an amount, usually accompanied by an expected acceptance, counteroffer, return promise, or act. A manifestation of willingness to enter into a bargain, so made as to justify another person in understanding that his assent to that bargain is invited and will conclude it.

Option Contract   Contract made for consideration to keep an offer open for prescribed period. A right, which acts as a continuing offer, given for consideration, to purchase or lease property at an agreed upon price and terms, within a specified time.

Output Contract   A contract in which one party agrees to sell his entire output and the other agrees to buy it; it is not illusory, though it may be indefinite. Such agreements are governed by UCC § 2-306.

P

Parol Evidence Rule   This evidence rule seeks to preserve integrity of written agreements by refusing to permit contracting parties to attempt to alter import of their contract through use of contemporaneous oral declarations. Under this rule when the parties to a contract embody their agreement in writing and intend the writing to be the final expression of their agreement, the terms of the writing may not be varied or contradicted by evidence of any prior written or oral agreement in the absence of fraud, duress, or mutual mistake. Also, as regards sales of goods, such written agreement may be explained or supplemented by course of dealing or usage of trade or by course of conduct, and by evidence of consistent additional terms, unless the court finds the writing to have been intended also as a complete and exclusive statement of the terms of the agreement (UCC § 2-202).

Performance   The fulfillment or accomplishment of a promise, contract, or other obligation according to its terms, relieving such person of all further obligation or liability thereunder.

Promissory Estoppel   That which arises when there is a promise, which promisor should reasonably expect to induce action or forbearance of a definite and substantial character on part of promisee, and which does induce such action or forbearance, and such promise is binding if injustice can be avoided only by enforcement of promise. Elements of a "promissory estoppel" are a promise clear and unambiguous in its terms, reliance by the party to whom the promise is made, with that reliance being both reasonable and foreseeable, and injury to the party asserting the estoppel as a result of his reliance.

Q

Quasi Contract Legal fiction invented by common law courts to permit recovery by contractual remedy in cases when, in fact, there is no contract, but when circumstances are such that justice warrants a recovery as though there had been a promise. It is not based on intention or consent of the parties, but is founded on considerations of justice and equity, and on doctrine of unjust enrichment.

R

Reformation A court-ordered correction of a written instrument to cause it to reflect the true intentions of the parties. Equitable remedy used to reframe written contracts to reflect accurately real agreement between contracting parties when, either through mutual mistake or unilateral mistake coupled with actual or equitable fraud by other party, the writing does not embody contract as actually made.

Repudiation Repudiation of contract is in nature of anticipatory breach before performance is due, but does not operate as anticipatory breach unless promisee elects to treat repudiation as breach, and brings suit for damages. Such repudiation is an act or declaration in advance of any actual breach and consists usually of absolute and unequivocal declaration or act amounting to declaration on part of promisor to promisee that he will not perform on future day that which contract calls for performance.

Requirements Contract A contract in which one party agrees to purchase his total requirements from the other party and hence it is binding and not illusory.

Rescission To abrogate, annul, avoid, or cancel a contract; particularly, nullifying a contract by the act of a party. The right of rescission is the right to cancel (rescind) a contract upon the occurrence of certain kinds of default by the other contracting party. To declare a contract void in its inception and to put an end to it, as though it never were.

Restitution An equitable remedy under which a person is restored to her original position prior to loss or injury, or placed in the position she would have been, had the breach not occurred.

Revocation In contract law, the withdrawal by the offeree of an offer that had been valid until withdrawn. The withdrawal of an offer by an offeror; unless the offer is irrevocable, it can be revoked at any time prior to acceptance without liability.

S

Specific Performance   The remedy of requiring exact performance of a contract in the specific form in which it was made, or according to the precise terms agreed upon. The actual accomplishment of a contract by a party bound to fulfill it. The doctrine of specific performance is that, when money damages would be an inadequate compensation for the breach of an agreement, the contractor or vendor will be compelled to perform specifically what he has agreed to do; e.g., ordered to execute a specific conveyance of land.

Statute of Frauds   Its chief characteristic is the provision that no suit or action shall be maintained on certain classes of contracts unless there shall be a note or memorandum thereof in writing signed by the party to be charged or by his authorized agent (e.g., contracts for the sale of goods priced at $500 or more; contracts for the sale of land; contracts which cannot, by their terms, be performed within a year; and contracts to guarantee the debt of another). UCC § 2-201 provides that a contract for the sale of goods for the price of $500 or more is not enforceable by way of action or defense unless there is some writing sufficient to indicate that a contract for sale has been made between the parties and signed by the party against whom enforcement is sought or by his authorized agent or broker.

Substantial Performance   A doctrine in commercial reasonableness which recognizes that the rendering of a performance which does not exactly meet the terms of the agreement (slight deviation) will be looked upon as fulfillment of the obligation, less the damages which result from any deviation from the promised performance.

Suretyship   The relationship among three parties whereby one person (the surety) guarantees payment of a debtor's debt owed to a creditor or acts as a co-debtor. Generally speaking, the relationship which exists when one person has undertaken an obligation and another person is also under an obligation or other duty to the obligee, who is entitled to but one performance, and as between the two who are bound, one rather than the other should perform.

T

Termination   With respect to a lease or contract, term refers to an ending, usually before the end of the anticipated term of the lease or contract, which termination may be by mutual agreement or may be by exercise of one party of one of his remedies due to the default of the other party.

Third-Party Beneficiary   One for whose benefit a promise is made in a contract but who is not a party to the contract. A prime requisite to the status of "third-party beneficiary" under a contract is that the parties to the contract must have intended to benefit the third party, who must be something more than a mere incidental beneficiary.

U

Unconscionability in Common Law   A doctrine under which courts may deny enforcement of unfair or oppressive contracts because of procedural abuses arising out of the contract formation, or because of substantive abuses relating to terms of the contract, such as terms which violate reasonable expectations of parties or which involve gross disparities in price; either abuse can be the basis for a finding of unconscionability. Basic test of "unconscionability" of contract is whether, under circumstances existing at time of making of contract and in light of general commercial background and commercial needs of particular trade or case, clauses involved are so one-sided as to oppress or unfairly surprise party. Unconscionability is generally recognized to include an absence of meaningful choice on the part of one of the parties to a contract, together with contract terms which are unreasonably favorable to the other party.

Unconscionability in Restatement of Contracts   If a contract or term thereof is unconscionable at the time the contract is made, a court may refuse to enforce the contract, or may enforce the remainder of the contract without the unconscionable term, or may so limit the application of any unconscionable term as to avoid any unconscionable result (R2d § 208).

Unconscionability in Uniform Commercial Code   (1) If the court as a matter of law finds the contract or any clause of the contract to have been unconscionable at the time it was made, the court may refuse to enforce the contract, or it may enforce the remainder of the contract without the unconscionable clause, or it may so limit the application of any unconscionable clause as to avoid any unconscionable result. (2) When it is claimed or appears to the court that the contract or any clause thereof may be unconscionable, the parties shall be afforded a reasonable opportunity to present evidence as to its commercial setting, purpose, and effect to aid the court in making the determination (UCC § 2-302).

Unconscionable   A contract, or a clause in a contract, that is so grossly unfair to one of the parties because of stronger bargaining powers of the other party; usually held to be void as against public policy. An unconscionable bargain or contract is one which no man in his senses, not under delusion, would make and which no fair and honest man would accept.

Undue Influence   Persuasion, pressure, or influence short of actual force, but stronger than mere advice, that so overpowers the dominated party's free will or judgment that he or she cannot act intelligently and voluntarily, but acts, instead, subject to the will or purposes of the dominating party.

Unenforceable Contract   An unenforceable contract is one for the breach of which neither the remedy of damages nor the remedy of specific performance is available, but which is recognized in some other way as creating a duty of performance, though there has been no ratification.

Uniform Commercial Code   One of the Uniform Laws drafted by the National Conference of Commissioners on Uniform State Laws and the American Law Institute governing commercial transactions, including sales and leasing of goods, transfer of funds, commercial paper, bank deposits and collections, letters of credit, bulk transfers, warehouse receipts, bills of lading, investment securities, and secured transactions. The UCC has been adopted in whole or substantially by all states.

Unilateral Contract   A unilateral contract is one in which one party makes an express engagement or undertakes a performance, without receiving in return any express engagement or promise of performance from the other.

Unilateral Mistake   A mistake or misunderstanding as to the terms or effect of a contract, made or entertained by one of the parties to it but not by the other.

V

Void Contract   A contract that does not exist at law; a contract having no legal force or binding effect.

Voidable Contract   A contract that is valid, but which may be legally voided at the option of one of the parties. One which is void as to wrongdoer but not void as to wronged party, unless he elects to so treat it.

W

Waiver   The intentional or voluntary relinquishment of a known right, or such conduct as warrants an inference of the relinquishment of such right, or when one dispenses with the performance of something he is entitled to exact or when one in possession of any right, whether conferred by law or by contract, with full knowledge of the material facts, does or forbears to do something the doing of which or the failure of forbearance to do which is inconsistent with the right, or his intention to rely upon it.

APPENDIX **C**

Table of Cases

APPENDIX C: TABLE OF CASES

Essay Test Questions and Model Answers

Essay I: Question

(30 Minutes)

Melody purchased a beautiful old home and decided to renovate the kitchen and two of the bedrooms. The bedrooms had identical dimensions, and Melody wanted them to have identical carpeting, wallpaper, and light fixtures. Chip, a local contractor, drew up some plans that Melody liked, and one morning they got together to discuss the project.

Chip told Melody, "I can tear out everything in the kitchen and put in all new floor covering, wallpaper, cabinets, and appliances. I'll also have to do some rewiring, and the total cost for the kitchen project will be $10,000. The bedrooms are not as complicated. They'll be $1,000." Melody, who had expected the price to be higher, was delighted. She told Chip to go ahead with the project.

Chip finished the bedrooms quickly and was halfway done with the kitchen when a friend of Melody's asked her whether the work was being done in compliance with the city's stringent new building code. Melody wasn't sure, and she asked the city to send out an inspector. The inspector found that Chip's rewiring work was not up to code and ordered that it be redone.

When Melody told Chip about the problem, he was upset. He told her, "Look, that new code is just ridiculous. I know they've set out these new standards and all, but I've been doing things this way for years and my work is perfectly safe. I'll have to add an additional $1,000 to the price if I'm gonna have to start over on the wiring. That'll bring the total cost of the project to $13,000."

Melody, who was startled by this, said, "Wait just a minute. I don't see why I should have to pay extra for you to follow the code. And even if I gave you another $1,000 the total would be $12,000." Chip responded, "Huh? It's $10,000 for the kitchen now, plus $1,000 for each of the bedrooms, so the total is $12,000. If we add another $1,000, it'll be $13,000."

Now Melody was angry, and she told Chip, "Where did you get $1,000 per bedroom. I thought the total price for both bedrooms was $1,000." Chip responded by telling her that the carpeting, wallpaper, and light fixtures for the two bedrooms cost well over $1,000, and when he added in labor he wasn't really making a dime on the bedroom part of the project.

After hearing this, Melody cooled down and said, "I guess I'll have to pay you the extra $1,000 for the rewiring, but I'll have to think about the bedroom situation."

Chip finished the project, and Melody consulted a lawyer. The lawyer told her that Chip was not entitled to the extra money for the kitchen and that he was also not entitled to more than $1,000 total for the two bedrooms. Based on this advice, Melody paid Chip only $11,000. If Chip files suit for the extra $2,000, what will be the likely outcome?

Worksheet

Essay I: Model Answer

With regard to the bedrooms, the problem is one of misunderstanding. Both parties adopted the phrase, "They'll be $1,000," but they attached materially different meanings to the words. Chip meant $1,000 per bedroom, and Melody meant a total of $1,000. To determine whether to enforce the contract and, if so, on whose terms, the court must examine each party's state of mind. The facts make it clear that neither party knew the other's meaning, but should they have known? Chip will point out that Melody was delighted by the price, suggesting that she must have suspected that there was something wrong with her interpretation. Melody will point out that Chip was the one who chose the ambiguous phrase, and he should have realized that it could cause confusion, particularly when heard by someone not familiar with construction costs.

If both parties should have known the other's meaning, or if neither party should have known, there is no contract at all regarding the bedrooms. This is not as drastic as it sounds, since Chip will then be entitled to restitution for the reasonable value of the goods and services he provided (up to a maximum of $2,000). If the court believes that one party should have known and the other party had no reason to know, the contract will be enforced according to the understanding of the party without reason to know. If that is Melody, she need only pay $1,000; if it is Chip, he will recover $2,000.

The rewiring presents a preexisting duty rule problem. Superficially, there appears to be consideration for Melody's promise to pay an additional $1,000. After all, Chip has agreed to make changes to the wiring in exchange for the extra money. When we look deeper, however, we find that the consideration may well have been illusory. Melody has a strong argument that Chip was under a duty as an implicit term of the original contract to make the work conform to the city code, and thus he has given nothing new at all. Under the traditional common law approach, this would make Melody's promise to pay extra money unenforceable.

More modern approaches offer Chip little relief. The Restatement (Second) of Contracts dispenses with the consideration requirement where the contract is executory on both sides (it is), there has been an unanticipated event, and the modification is fair and equitable in light of that event. Here there has been no unanticipated event—the city code was in effect at the time of the original deal, and Chip knew it. Even the UCC (which would have to be applied by analogy to this service contract) is unlikely to be helpful to Chip. While the UCC dispenses with the consideration requirement for modifications, it subjects them to a good faith test. Chip will have a tough time convincing a court that his conduct in ignoring the city code and then charging a premium when he is caught amounts to good faith.

Essay II: Question

(60 Minutes)

Jerry owned a large tract of land that fronted on one of the main thoroughfares of his city. The whole area was developing rapidly, and Jerry wanted to cash in on the business boom. Accordingly, he hired Chip as his real estate agent and told Chip that he would pay a 6 percent commission if Chip could obtain a contract with a buyer willing to pay at least $500,000 for the land. The contract made it clear that Jerry would not be liable to Chip if he (Jerry) located a prospective purchaser and entered into a contract to sell the land to that person before Chip could complete his performance. Chip went right to work, placing ads in the local newspapers, spreading the word among other realtors, and showing the property to prospective buyers.

Phil had recently been fired from his job as a law professor because he gave his first-year students sufficient time to complete his torts exam. Phil had received severance pay from the university and was looking for a new line of work. His dream was to own a clothing-store franchise, but he didn't want to be obligated to buy it. Eventually, Phil and Jerry worked out a deal whereby Phil was given a sixty-day option to purchase the land for a total price of $600,000. In order to exercise the option, Phil had to notify Jerry of his intentions on or before the sixtieth day. Because the price Phil was willing to pay was so high, Jerry didn't insist on any payment for the option period. Nevertheless, the contract, which was signed by both parties, stated that the option had been given "for a good and valuable consideration." Jerry was aware that Phil needed the option period in order to secure a franchise agreement.

After nailing down the option, Phil set out to secure a franchise. He called Nanette, the president of Punks 'R Us. Punks was riding the crest of the grunge wave and opening stores all across America at a frantic pace. Nanette was interested in the Columbia market, and she flew out with her lawyers to hammer out a deal with Phil. The standard Punks's contract contained the following terms:

1. Phil could use the name "Punks 'R Us" at his store and in his advertising. In return, Phil had to pay Punks a fee equal to 8 percent of his gross sales.

2. Punks would make its complete line of clothing available to Phil for sale at his store. Punks would supply all of Phil's needs for clothing at its standard wholesale price, and any unsold clothing could be returned by Phil for a 98 percent refund.

3. Phil would hire a local contractor and build the store according to Punks's standard architectural design.

4. At the end of each year, Phil would receive a fair and reasonable bonus if, in Nanette's opinion, his efforts during the year warranted a bonus.

Phil had no trouble with any of the terms other than the 8 percent fee. After studying the situation with his accountant, he concluded that he could not make a go of it if he was obligated to a fee of that magnitude. He tried to negotiate a better deal, but Nanette was adamant. Reluctantly, Phil gave up on Punks. He was so upset by the situation that he considered not becoming a clothier after all. On the fiftieth day of the option period, he called Jerry and stated, "Things look pretty bad for me. It looks like I may not be able to go through with the deal after all."

Jerry was secretly delighted by Phil's decision. He had received an offer of $650,000 for the land from Lisa, whom he had located personally. After talking to Phil, Jerry tried to call Lisa to accept the offer, but she was not in. Jerry left a message on her recorder asking that she call him as soon as possible.

While Jerry was trying to get hold of Lisa, Nanette had a change of heart. She concluded that Columbia would be a booming market for years to come and that she could live with a lower fee for a while in order to help Phil get off the ground. She called Phil and told him that she would accept a fee of 3 percent for the first two years and 5 percent for the next two years. At the end of the fourth year, the parties would negotiate a permanent fee structure. Phil agreed at once, and he and Nanette exchanged faxes consummating the deal.

Phil was elated and called Jerry at once. He said, "Jerry, it's just the fifty-first day of my option period, and I've had some interesting things happen." He was about to go on when Jerry stopped him and said, "Hold on just a minute there. I'm going to sell the land to Lisa." At just that moment, Jerry's other line rang, and he asked Phil to hold on for a moment. When Jerry answered the other line, it was Lisa. Jerry quickly accepted her offer and then switched back to Phil. "Phil," he said, "I've got a contract with Lisa and there's nothing you can do about it." Phil was furious and shouted, "Oh no you don't. I am hereby placing you on notice that I am exercising my option. The land is mine. If you back out I'll have to breach my contract with Punks, and I'm not about to let that happen. Who knows how high my liability might be." Jerry, however, refused to sell the land to Phil and instead conveyed title to Lisa. Phil had to call Nanette and tell her that the deal was off, and Nanette informed Phil that her lawyers would prepare a suit against him to recover the damages caused by his breach. Meanwhile, Chip learned what had occurred and demanded that Jerry pay him 6 percent of the $600,000 that Phil had been willing to pay.

Did Jerry incur any liability to Phil when he sold the land to Lisa? Is Jerry liable to Chip for the 6 percent commission? Is Phil liable to Nanette for any damages caused to Punks? Is this whole thing a mess, or what?

Worksheet

Essay II: Model Answer

1. Is Jerry liable to Phil? Jerry's offer to Phil may or may not have been irrevocable. Phil gave no consideration for the option period, not even nominal consideration, and under traditional common law principles (and the law of most jurisdictions) the offer would be freely revocable. Under the Restatement (Second) of Contracts, however, a signed writing that "recites" a consideration creates a binding option contract. Whether a true option contract was created, then, turns on the law of the jurisdiction.

If the offer is revocable, there is no contract. Phil's statement to Jerry on the fiftieth day was equivocal and therefore probably not a rejection, but Jerry notified Phil that he had sold the land to Lisa before Phil could accept, thereby revoking the offer. If the offer is irrevocable, however, there is a contract between Phil and Jerry.

Even if Phil did not create a true option contract under the law of the jurisdiction, he can argue that Jerry was estopped to revoke the offer because of Phil's reliance in entering into the contract with Nanette. Jerry was aware that Phil would be seeking such a contract, making Phil's reliance foreseeable.

2. Is Phil obligated to Nanette? Phil can try to avoid the contract because of (1) indefiniteness of the "fair and reasonable bonus" term and (2) unenforceability due to the agreement to agree on future percentages.

With regard to the indefiniteness problem, the contract can be avoided only if the term at issue is material and there is no objective basis for filling the gap. There is no information in the problem regarding the importance of the bonus to parties, but any compensation term is likely to be considered material. The real issue here is whether there is an objective basis for filling the gap. Since this is part of the standard Punks contract, there may be a track record of Nanette's practices with regard to other franchisees. The issue of whether a court will refuse to enforce the contract on this basis is a close one.

As to the agreement to agree, there are still a few jurisdictions that simply will not enforce such arrangements, although most of the modern decisions to that effect involve land contracts. It will be difficult for Nanette to recover damages for the "out years" (after the first four years) because such damages would be speculative, but unless agreements to agree are unenforceable as a matter of law in the jurisdiction, the clause will not preclude a recovery for lost profits during the first four years.

3. Is Jerry liable to Chip? Offers to real estate agents are historically viewed as offers for unilateral contracts and acceptance must be by full performance. Full performance required

that Chip's prospect enter into a contract with Jerry before Jerry could enter into a contract with a prospect that he had developed. Under this analysis, Chip's right to a fee turns on Phil's right to enforce a contract against Jerry. If Phil had an enforceable option contract (whether created by estoppel or otherwise), then Jerry was not at liberty to sell to Lisa. Phil could not wrongfully prevent Chip from performing and earning his fee. Since Phil accepted Jerry's offer, a contract was formed and Chip is entitled to his fee.

If, on the other hand, there was no option contract, then Jerry had every right under his contract with Chip to sell the land to Lisa. Since Jerry entered into a contract with Lisa before Phil accepted, he would not be liable for the fee.

Essay III: Question

(30 Minutes)

Film director Pocus Fuller decided he needed some old cars to use in the background of a street scene in the Prohibition-era epic he had begun filming. He telephoned Kitty Karr, owner of Karr's Klassic Kars, and explained that in particular he wanted to buy two old cars painted in taxicab livery to park on the street where a gunfight would take place. These cars would be essentially destroyed by gunfire during the filming. Kitty said to Pocus, who knew very little about old cars, "I have just what you need. I will sell you two 1928 Whitney taxicabs for $1,000 apiece. I can have my truck deliver them at 9:00 A.M. tomorrow in plenty of time for your filming the day after tomorrow. I guarantee that you will love them." Amazed at the incredibly low price, Pocus said, "I accept your offer."

Without further communication, the cars showed up at 9:00 A.M. as scheduled, and the truck driver dropped them off on the street where filming was to be done the next day. Pocus promptly sent Kitty a check for $2,000, accompanied by a note stating, "Thanks for sending the cars as per our discussion yesterday."

By chance, Pocus discovered just after the two Whitneys were delivered that although they looked identical to the 1928 models, they were in fact 1935 models built well after Prohibition had ended and thus were not authentic. Furthermore, they had no engines. Because Pocus was on a tight production schedule, he decided to go ahead and use the cars the next day, but to film the gunfight using special effects rather than actually shooting up the cars with live ammunition. Pocus's intention was to return the cars to Kitty after the filming and demand a refund. The cost of the special effects was $2,000; to delay filming while other genuine 1928 Whitneys were located would have cost $20,000 per day.

The special effects method worked fine for one of the cars, which emerged undamaged; unfortunately, the special effects went awry as to the second car and it was completely destroyed.

Pocus shipped both the undamaged car and the burned-out hulk of the other one back to Kitty and demanded satisfaction, stating, "First, these are 1935 Whitneys, not 1928 ones; second, they do not have engines, and thus do not qualify as 'cars'; and third, I definitely do not 'love' these cars, and you guaranteed that I would." Kitty did not respond.

Discuss fully the likely result of Pocus's suit against Kitty for breach of contract.

Worksheet

Essay III: Model Answer

Pocus probably will not recover anything in his suit against Kitty because he did not follow the proper course of action upon being tendered nonconforming goods.

The transaction between Pocus and Kitty will be controlled by Article 2 of the Uniform Commercial Code, since it involves a sale of goods. Goods are defined as things movable at the time of identification to the sales contract, with certain exceptions such as investment securities. The Whitney taxicabs thus qualify as goods, and the transaction involves their sale, as opposed to some other type of transfer such as a lease or a gift.

The transaction appears to amount to an enforceable contract, aside from the issue of breach, discussed below. An enforceable contract, whether under Article 2 or not, at a minimum requires an offer, an acceptance, and consideration or a substitute for consideration. Here, Kitty offered to sell two 1928 Whitney taxicabs to Pocus, Pocus accepted, and Pocus paid $2,000 as consideration. As a general rule, under UCC § 2-201(1)—the UCC's "Statute of Frauds" provision—a contract for the sale of goods for more than $500 is not enforceable unless it is in writing, but exceptions exist. An exception to the UCC's Statute of Frauds exists where the goods have been accepted and paid for. Here, Kitty shipped the cars to Pocus and Pocus sent a check for the full price to Kitty. Thus, it is too late to claim that no enforceable contract exists on the basis of there being no sufficient writing.

Pocus's best claim against Kitty, had he acted properly with respect to the taxicabs, would have been to assert a breach of the UCC's "perfect tender rule," as embodied in UCC § 2-601. Under this section, if the goods delivered "fail in any respect to conform to the contract," the buyer may reject the whole shipment, accept the whole shipment, or accept any commercial units and reject the rest. It is uncertain whether Pocus could have prevailed on the basis of the perfect tender rule regarding the fact that the cars had no engines, since there may have been some ambiguity here. That is, Kitty might argue that her reasonable understanding of the parties' agreement was that the cars need not have engines, since the cars, used as movie props, were to be parked on a street and destroyed. Kitty might further argue that Pocus should have realized that the bargain price she charged him meant that the cars would not have engines. Regardless of how the court ruled on the no-engine issue, Pocus certainly could have rejected both taxicabs upon discovering that they were the wrong model year, since the contract explicitly called for 1928 Whitneys, not 1935 ones. It is immaterial for purposes of the perfect tender rule that the two model years looked identical.

Before Pocus could assert the perfect tender rule, he must show that he acted in accord with the requirements of Article 2 upon being shipped nonconforming goods. UCC § 2-508 describes a seller's right to cure: where a buyer rejects nonconforming goods and the time for performance has not yet expired, the seller may cure the nonconformity within the remaining time. Thus, if Pocus wanted to hold Kitty liable for the cars' nonconformity, he should have notified her that he intended to reject them, upon which Kitty might have been able to supply genuine 1928 Whitneys. It appears that time remained for her to do so, since filming was not to take place until the next day.

Under UCC § 2-606, acceptance of tendered goods occurs when the buyer fails to reject goods after inspection or does something inconsistent with the seller's continued ownership. A buyer may later revoke acceptance of nonconforming goods whose nonconformity substantially impairs their value to him if he accepted them on the assumption that the nonconformity would be cured or if he did not discover the nonconformity and his acceptance was induced by the difficulty of discovering the nonconformity or by the seller's assurances. Revocation of acceptance must occur within a reasonable time after the buyer discovers the nonconformity and before any substantial change in the condition of the goods. In Pocus's case, because he did not reject the cars or notify Kitty of their nonconformity so that she might cure it, he thereby "accepted" the cars. It is probably too late for him to revoke his acceptance. First, it might be argued that the fact that the Whitneys were 1935 models did not "substantially impair their value," since they looked exactly like the 1928 models. Second, at least as to the car that was destroyed in the filming, a substantial change in the condition of the goods has taken place.

Pocus might argue that his actions with respect to the cars were motivated by his desire to mitigate his damages, since it would have been very costly to delay filming. The flaw in this argument is, as discussed above, that he never gave Kitty an opportunity to cure the nonconforming tender within the time remaining. He thus accepted the goods, nonconformity and all, and cannot now reject them.

Finally, Pocus also will not prevail in arguing that he did not "love" the cars as Kitty promised he would. First, the court might interpret Kitty's statement as "puffery," i.e., somewhat exaggerated statements touting the value of the goods but not meant to be taken literally. Second, even if the court interpreted Kitty's statement as one of "satisfaction guaranteed," the court would probably apply an objective standard. That is, especially in commercial settings for matters not involving personal taste, the court will determine whether a reasonable person would have been satisfied. Here, the court would determine that a reasonable person buying cars to use in a movie would have been satisfied with 1935 cars that looked exactly like the 1928 cars.

Essay IV: Question

(60 Minutes)

Farmer Lomy Fields is always looking to expand his land holdings and has considered several parcels.

(a) First, Lomy had his eye on the 40-acre parcel owned by Marnie Silo. Marnie offered to sell Lomy the land for $200,000. Knowing that this price was ridiculously high by prevailing standards, Lomy wrote back to her, "Oh, sure. If I ever inherit a million dollars, I'll buy that land for $200,000." Marnie then sold the parcel to Rich Soils for $100,000, its true market price. Two years later, Lomy's aunt Tillie Fields died and left Lomy a million dollars. Marnie showed Lomy's letter to Rich. Rich tendered title to Lomy, demanding $200,000.

Discuss fully the likely result of Rich's suit against Lomy for specific performance.

(b) Lomy suspected Cassie Legume might be willing to sell the 40-acre Legume Farm. He telephoned Cassie and they agreed on a price of $125,000. At the end of this conversation, Lomy said, "I think our deal should be in writing. Send me a contract in the mail and I'll mail it back to you." Cassie mailed a document to Lomy that said,

> I, Cassie Legume, offer to sell to Lomy Fields the 40 acres legally known as Legume Farm for $125,000, closing to be had within 7 days.
>
> signed: [Cassie Legume]
> accepted: _____

Cassie deposited this document in the mail on Monday. On the same day, before receiving Cassie's missive, Lomy decided that $125,000 was too much, and mailed to Cassie a document stating, "I decline to buy Legume Farm for $125,000, but I would buy Legume Farm for $115,000; in fact, by this letter I accept any offer you might make to sell Legume Farm for $115,000 cash." Cassie, having been suspicious all along of the legitimacy of Lomy's intentions, had as a backup to Lomy advertised Legume Farm for sale in the weekly agricultural newspaper for $115,000. Lomy never saw this ad. By Wednesday, all the relevant mail had been delivered, and Lomy had decided that he did not want Legume Farm after all. He telephoned Cassie and informed her of his decision.

Discuss fully the likely result of a suit by Cassie against Lomy for specific performance.

(c) Pops Ballon also had a 40-acre parcel for sale. It had been on the market for months at a bargain price of $40,000. Lomy called Pops and told him, "I'll buy your 40 acres for $40,000 cash. We can close the deal next Monday if that's okay." Pops assured Lomy that he would tender clear title to the 40 acres on Monday. Pops then wrote to his son, Lud Ballon, about the deal, specifying in his letter, "When this deal closes, I'll give you the $20,000 you need to buy that exquisite pre-Raphaelite widget you've been wanting. If I were you, I'd lock in that price before it goes up." Lud agreed that this was a good idea, and contracted with the widget's owner to buy it on Tuesday for $20,000. Lomy then began to wonder why Pops was selling the land so cheaply. Lomy called Pops and said, "I just don't feel right about this. The deal's off." Pops, realizing that he had been offering his land too cheaply, did not pursue the matter, and began seeking another buyer at a higher price.

Discuss fully the likely result of Lud's suit against Lomy based on a third-party beneficiary theory, and his suit against Pops based on a reliance theory.

Worksheet

Essay IV: Model Answer

(a) Rich is unlikely to succeed in his suit for specific performance against Lomy for several reasons.

First, Marnie herself probably could not have prevailed in an action against Lomy, either for specific performance or for damages, because Lomy did not truly assent to her offer. Central to formation of a contract is the concept of mutual assent. Intent to form a contract is ordinarily judged by an objective standard; that is, what a reasonable person in the place of the recipient of the communication would interpret the words to mean. Here, a reasonable person would probably understand from the sarcastic tone of Lomy's written reply that he did not really intend to be bound by the literal meaning of his words.

Second, Lomy could assert that his letter was not an acceptance; it was a counteroffer to Marnie and could only be accepted by her. Marnie, if she still owned the land and was the one attempting to enforce the contract, would argue that an acceptance was created the moment Lomy inherited a million dollars. Lomy would argue that no such acceptance was created, since his letter to Marnie attached a condition and that therefore his "acceptance" violated the mirror image rule. According to this rule, an acceptance must accept the offer exactly as presented. That is, Lomy would argue that his "acceptance" varied the offer by asking Marnie to wait until he inherited a million dollars. It therefore constituted a counteroffer. As a general rule, an offer (including a counteroffer) may be accepted only by the specific offeree to whom it is made. Here, Lomy's counteroffer, in the unlikely event it is found to be serious, was made to Marnie. It therefore could not be accepted by Rich.

Finally, Lomy could argue that his counteroffer terminated through lapse of time. Whether sufficient time has elapsed so as to terminate an offer is a question of fact and varies with the subject matter and circumstances of the offer. Here, the subject matter is real estate and the language of the counteroffer ("If I ever . . . ") suggests that a long time period was envisioned. On the other hand, and probably dispositive of the issue, Lomy would probably be entitled to consider his offer terminated when Marnie sold the land to Rich and thus incapacitated herself from accepting Lomy's offer, at least not without Rich's cooperation in selling the land back to her first.

In the unlikely event Rich prevailed for some reason, he would probably be entitled to specific performance by Lomy. Most courts will grant specific performance in favor of the seller where the buyer breaches a contract for the sale of land. Traditionally, this was based on the doctrine of mutuality of remedy; more recently, the rationale has been that money damages are inadequate to a seller left with incidental expenses (taxes, maintenance, etc.) of continuing to own land he expected to sell. Thus, if Rich prevailed, Lomy would probably be required to buy the land for $200,000.

(b) Cassie is not entitled to specific performance or damages from Lomy, since no enforceable contract was ever created. This result derives from the correct characterization of the various communications between Cassie and Lomy.

First, Lomy's telephone agreement with Cassie is not enforceable, since a contract for the sale of land must be in writing in order to satisfy the Statute of Frauds. Furthermore, Lomy specifically indicated his intent not to be bound until the agreement was in writing.

The document Cassie sent to Lomy is by its terms an offer, even though Lomy asked that Cassie send him a "contract," and even though Cassie might now wish to characterize the document as her signed "acceptance" of Lomy's previously telephoned offer. Cassie's desired characterization of the writing will fail, however, since it is not signed by the person to be charged, namely Lomy. As a mere offer, this document has no legal significance as a contract for the sale of Legume Farm; had Lomy signed it and deposited it in the mail, his acceptance would have been effective on dispatch and a contract would have been formed.

Lomy's next communication to Cassie—the document stating that he declined to buy Legume Farm for $125,000 but "accepting" any offer she might make to sell it for $115,000—is in fact an offer, even though it calls itself an acceptance. The reason for this is that Cassie has not yet made a true offer to sell Legume Farm for $115,000; a newspaper ad such as the one Cassie placed in the local agricultural paper is ordinarily construed as an invitation to make offers. Cassie did not accept Lomy's offer before it was revoked by his telephone call telling her he had decided not to buy Legume Farm after all.

Because neither party effectively accepted an offer by the other, no contract exists and Cassie therefore cannot prevail.

(c) Lud will not prevail against either Lomy or Pops.

Under the terminology of the First Restatement, which most courts follow, third-party beneficiaries are donee beneficiaries, creditor beneficiaries, or incidental beneficiaries. A donee beneficiary is a third person to whom the promisee intended to make a gift or to confer a right against the promisor to a performance not owed to the third person by the promisee. The Second Restatement classifies third-party beneficiaries as either intended or incidental. This scheme essentially combines the First Restatement's concepts of donee and creditor beneficiaries and calls them intended beneficiaries. Thus, under the First Restatement, Lud would argue that he is a donee beneficiary, since Pops intended to make a gift to him of $20,000 of the proceeds of Pops's contract with Lomy; and under the Second Restatement, Lud would argue that he is an intended beneficiary.

A third-party beneficiary's right to enforce a contract against a promisor depends on whether the beneficiary's right has vested. A majority of courts consider that vesting occurs when the third-party beneficiary learns of the contract and assents to it, materially changes his position in justified reliance on the promise, or sues to enforce the promise. The promisor may, however, assert as defenses against the beneficiary any defenses the promisor could have asserted against the promisee.

Here, Lud will not prevail against Lomy, since Lomy could have asserted against Pops the defense of the Statute of Frauds. The Statute of Frauds requires that contracts for the sale of land be in writing, and no writing appears to have been executed between Pops and Lomy. Since Lomy wishes to avoid the oral agreement he made with Pops, if Pops had chosen to pursue enforcement of the contract, Lomy could have asserted the Statute of Frauds as a defense. Lomy may assert this same defense against Lud, and Lud thus cannot prevail.

If Lud proceeds against Pops on a theory of reliance, Lud will also fail. Lud will argue that he detrimentally relied—by contracting to buy the widget for $20,000—on Pops's promise to give him that amount when Pops's deal with Lomy closed.

Pops's promise to pay $20,000 to Lud is, absent other factors, a gift. As a general rule, promises to make a gift are not enforceable as contracts because the contractual requirement of consideration is absent. Detrimental reliance by the donee on the gift may serve as a substitute for consideration where:

1. it was foreseeable to the promisor that the promisee would rely on receiving the gift;

2. the promisee did rely; and

3. injustice can be avoided only by enforcing the promise.

Initially, these factors appear to have been met in Lud's case, since it was foreseeable to Pops that Lud would "lock in" the $20,000 price for the widget (in fact, Pops encouraged him to do so). Lud made the contract with the widget seller as Pops suggested, and it now seems unjust to allow Pops to escape this promise.

Pops will argue, however, that his promise of a gift to Lud was subject to a condition precedent; namely, that the deal with Lomy closed. A condition precedent is one that must occur before the obligation to which it is attached becomes an absolute duty. Pops's agreement with Lud stated, "When this deal closes, I'll give you the $20,000. . . ." Thus, on the face of it, closing of the deal with Lomy was a condition precedent to Pops's obligation to perform.

Lud will counter with the argument that the party whose obligation is subject to a condition may not prevent the occurrence of the condition. Pops, Lud will argue, caused the condition to fail by not pursuing enforcement of his contract with Lomy in court. As a general rule, however, a court will not require a party to perform a useless act, and it would appear useless to require that Pops sue Lomy when Lomy both has indicated his desire to avoid the contract and has the defense of the Statute of Frauds readily available to him.

Essay V: Question

(60 Minutes)

The village of Muddy Fen is encouraging public and private beautification efforts in anticipation of its upcoming bicentennial celebration on May 15.

(a) Muddy Fen contracted with Violet Mulch to prepare the flower beds around the village hall for planting for $2,000. This job consisted of manual labor requiring no particular skill. Muddy Fen paid Violet $2,000, and she in turn contracted with Dan DeLeon to do the actual work for $1,500. Dan did a cursory job and the flower beds were soon covered with weeds. The mayor of Muddy Fen called Violet and complained. Violet said, "Hey, pal, I delegated this contract in a perfectly legal manner. There's no no-assignment clause, and there's no change in your obligation nor any element of personal service. Sue me. Your complaint is with Dan DeLeon. Goodbye." Muddy Fen sued Violet for $2,000.

Discuss fully the likely result of Muddy Fen's suit against Violet.

(b) Ray O'Sunstein had several large shady areas in his yard and wanted to cover them with hosta plants, which thrive in the shade. He mailed a note to Esther Hester, owner of Hester's Hostas, and asked for "100 of them Mexican hostas you have." Esther sold two varieties of hosta from Mexico: Mañana hostas, which have striped leaves, and La Vista baby hostas, which have solid color leaves. Esther recalled Ray having visited her store last week just before she received her first shipment of Mañana hostas, so she thought Ray did not know about them and must have been talking about La Vista baby hostas. Esther wrote back to Ray that she would sell him 100 "Mexican hostas" for $600. Ray in fact had meant Mañana hostas, since he had heard from his neighbor the day before he wrote to Esther that she had just received a shipment of them.

Esther shipped 100 La Vista baby hostas to Ray, who was an amateur gardener and did not know one hosta from another. Ray paid for and planted the La Vista baby hostas, and by midsummer they grew into stunningly beautiful mature specimens. As it turned out, Mañana hostas this year were subject to a blight and would have died. Ray's neighbor came by and said, "It's a good thing you didn't take my advice about the Mañana hostas." Ray then realized for the first time that he had been shipped the wrong hostas.

Discuss fully the likely result of Ray's suit against Esther for $600.

(c) Gene Mutanté, a homeowner on Polyethyl Lane in Muddy Fen, always had difficulty maintaining a nice lawn, so he contracted with Myrtle Crescent to have her maintain it. Myrtle guaranteed that for $1,500 her techniques would produce an emerald green, weed-free lawn within three months, and that she would maintain the lawn in that condition for the three following years at an annual cost of $500. Myrtle told Gene she would use her proven techniques of diligently watering, mowing, and weeding the lawn and judiciously applying various chemicals. Two weeks before the three-month deadline was up, the lawn looked worse than ever. Looking through some old newspapers, Myrtle discovered that Polyethyl Lane, and in fact all of Volatile Rivers subdivision, was built on an old chemical waste dump shortly after World War II. Myrtle conducted soil tests and discovered contamination from the surface down to at least 15 feet. The contamination made growing any kind of plants difficult, much less an emerald green lawn. Furthermore, Myrtle discovered that the interaction between the contaminated soil and the chemicals she applied actually made the situation worse.

The only thing that could be done for Gene's lawn within the two weeks remaining on the contractual three-month period was to replace all the topsoil to a depth of two feet and to install new sod on top of that, at a total cost of $30,000. Even with this remedy, Myrtle estimated, the contamination would percolate to the surface again within two years and the process would have to be repeated. Myrtle told Gene that she refused to perform this season's part of the contract for $1,500 and certainly would not do it within the remaining two weeks.

Gene sued for specific performance; alternatively, he sought $60,000, which represented the cost of replacing the topsoil and sod two times in the next four years, at $30,000 each time.

Discuss fully the likely result of Gene's suit.

(d) The village of Muddy Fen, inclined to give Violet Mulch another chance (see part (a) above), subsequently contracted with her to prepare the flowerbeds around the sewage treatment plant for another $2,000. Violet called the village office and said she was too busy and wondered if the village would mind if Forsythia Amarilla did the work instead. Forsythia had an excellent reputation, and Violet's own reputation had been damaged by the events described in part (a), so the village was inclined to go along with Violet's plan. The village called Forsythia to ask about the deal. Forsythia said, "I'll send you a document explaining it all." Forsythia then sent a letter to Muddy Fen saying, "As Violet explained to you, I'll be doing the sewage plant flowerbed preparation instead of Violet. I expect to be paid the price you arranged with Violet, half up front and half on completion. If this is acceptable, please sign the enclosed contract reflecting these terms and send me a check for $1,000. As you can see, Violet has also signed this agreement. You should probably also know that her profit on this deal is $250, since I will be paying her that amount as a 'finder's fee' for this contract." The appropriate Muddy Fen village official signed the document and sent it to Forsythia with a check for $1,000.

Forsythia was never heard from again. With the sewage plant's flowerbeds unprepared by May 14, the village hired another contractor to do the work for $3,000. The village then noticed that its contract with Violet had included a standard boilerplate no-assignment clause, so it sued Violet for $2,000, which represented the $1,000 it had sent Forsythia plus the $1,000 increase in price it had paid to the substitute contractor at the last minute.

Discuss fully the likely result of Muddy Fen's suit against Violet.

Worksheet

Essay V: Model Answer

(a) Muddy Fen is likely to prevail against Violet, who appears to be confusing the concepts of assignment of contract rights and delegation of contract duties.

Each party to a contract has both rights and duties: the *right* to performance by the other party, and the *duty* to perform himself. In proper circumstances, rights can be assigned and duties can be delegated. After a contract has been formed, an assignment of rights occurs where one of the original contracting parties (the assignor) transfers to a third person (the assignee) the assignor's right to the performance of the other original contracting party (the obligor). A delegation occurs where one of the original contracting parties (the obligor) transfers his duty to perform for the other contracting party (the obligee) to a third person (the delegatee). Where an entire contract is transferred, there may be both an assignment and a delegation. Thus, for example, if Violet had both hired Dan to do the work and told Muddy Fen to pay the $2,000 to Dan, both a delegation and an assignment would have occurred. As it is, however, only a delegation has occurred: Violet (the obligor) transferred her duty to perform for Muddy Fen (the obligee) to Dan (the delegatee).

The specific issue as to which Violet is mistaken concerns her own continuing duty as obligor. That is, where an obligor delegates to another person her duty to perform, the obligor remains liable to the obligee for the proper completion of the performance. Thus, Violet's duty to perform under the original contract is not discharged until Dan performs satisfactorily. If Dan performs improperly, Muddy Fen may recover damages from Violet for breach of contract.

Violet is otherwise correct that the delegation appears to be "perfectly legal." As her comment suggests, delegation is normally proper in the absence of a contract provision prohibiting it and where there is no element of personal service, such as would be the case if the work involved a particular skill, artistic taste, etc. Violet's contract involves manual labor described as requiring no particular skill. Violet's reference to the absence of a no-assignment clause is irrelevant since, as discussed, no assignment has taken place. (The contract apparently also did not contain a clause prohibiting delegation.)

Finally, Violet's comment about "no change in your obligation" refers to a concept relevant to assignment, not delegation. The principle to which she refers states that an original contracting party may not assign to another his right to performance by the other original contracting party (the obligor) if the assignment would increase the obligor's burden of performance. For example, X's contractual right to use Y's car cannot be assigned (absent permission) to Z, since Z may be a poor driver.

(b) Ray will not prevail in his suit against Esther.

The transaction between Ray and Esther will be governed by Article 2 of the Uniform Commercial Code, since it involves a contract for the sale of goods. Goods are, in general, things movable at the time of their identification to the contract for their sale. This definition includes most growing things, such as crops or timber, that may be severed without damage to the real property. Landscape plants, such as the hostas at issue here, that have already been severed from the land and are in transplantable form are well within the definition of goods.

The subject matter of Ray's and Esther's contract was identified by them as "Mexican hostas." Ray and Esther, however, each attached a different meaning to the term. The situation thus resembles the famous *Peerless* case, in which the two parties to a purported contract, in which transportation on the ship *Peerless* was a critical element, each intended a different ship called the *Peerless*. The *Peerless* case held that no contract was formed, since there was no mutual assent. Thus, were it not for the UCC, the court in Ray's case would take the view that no contract had been formed, and Ray would have been left to his restitutionary remedy, if any.

While the UCC has no provision directly addressing *Peerless*-type instances of failure of mutual assent, other provisions of Article 2 relating to acceptance and rejection of tendered goods indicate that Ray has missed his chance to reject nonconforming goods. UCC § 2-601 of the UCC embodies a "perfect tender rule" that gives a buyer the right to reject goods that fail to conform to the contract in any respect. Even after accepting goods, a buyer may, pursuant to UCC § 2-608, revoke his acceptance of goods whose nonconformity substantially impairs their value to him if he believed the nonconformity would be cured and it was not, or if he failed to discover a nonconformity because it was reasonably undiscoverable or because he was lulled by the seller's assurances. A revocation of acceptance under UCC § 2-608 must occur within a reasonable time after the buyer discovers or should have discovered the nonconformity, and there can be no substantial change in the condition of the goods not caused by their own defectiveness.

In Ray's case, it is too late to revoke acceptance, even if the court found that the La Vista baby hostas did not conform to the contract for "Mexican" hostas. First, Ray's failure to discover the nonconformity is due entirely to his own inexpertise, and cannot be charged to Esther. That is, he "should have discovered" the nonconformity upon noting that the hostas he received had solid-color leaves. (This assumes that at no point did Esther "lull" Ray by assuring him that the hostas were in fact the Mañana variety.) Second, Ray has simply waited well beyond the "reasonable" time allowed by Article 2. Not only did he plant the hostas; he also waited several weeks until they had grown into mature specimens—thus bringing about a "substantial change in the condition of the goods"—before he discovered the problem and complained.

Thus, Ray has accepted the goods and can no longer revoke his acceptance even though from his point of view they are nonconforming.

(c) Gene is unlikely to obtain the relief he seeks against Myrtle since Myrtle's duty to perform has probably been discharged by impracticability.

The transaction between Gene and Myrtle will be controlled by the common law rather than Article 2 of the UCC, since it is primarily a contract for services, even though goods (the chemicals) are incidentally involved.

The doctrine of discharge by impracticability has grown out of the doctrine of discharge by impossibility. Where performance of contractual duties has become impossible—as by death where a contract calls for performance by a particular person, or by destruction of the subject matter without fault or assumption of the risk by either party—the duty to perform is discharged. More recently, courts have recognized that impossibility is not an all-or-nothing phenomenon, and have allowed discharge in certain circumstances where a contract could theoretically be performed, but only at great expense or difficulty. The expense or difficulty must be extreme, however; in the classic cases the courts refused to apply the doctrine in circumstances where closure of the Suez Canal forced oil tankers to use the much more costly route around Africa.

With respect to the contract between Gene and Myrtle, Myrtle's total cost of performance, not counting what she has already expended, would be $60,000 over 4 years. This is 20 times the contract price of $1,500 now plus $1,500 over the next 3 years, and is probably a sufficiently extreme example of increased expense of performance to give rise to discharge by impracticability. This is especially so in light of the fact that after all this expense, the contaminated condition apparently would recur in future years.

Another possible approach Myrtle might take in seeking to have her duty discharged would be to argue mutual mistake. Mutual mistake is a defense to formation of a contract, since it indicates that the requisite mutual assent is lacking. That is, if both parties to a purported contract are mistaken about a material aspect of the subject matter, mutual assent cannot exist. For this defense to apply, the party seeking to assert it must not have assumed the risk that both parties are mistaken.

In the transaction between Gene and Myrtle, both parties apparently entered the agreement under the assumption that the soil under Gene's lawn was no different from other soil in the area upon which Myrtle's techniques had worked. Nothing about the agreement or the surrounding circumstances indicates that Myrtle assumed the risk that the soil might be extensively contaminated, so she may argue that no contract was ever formed.

(d) This time, Violet will prevail and will not be held liable, since a novation has occurred.

In a delegation, as discussed in part (a), the original obligor remains liable under the contract until the delegatee satisfactorily performs. The reason for this is that in a delegation the obligee has not agreed to release the obligor from performance. In a novation, the obligee agrees to release the obligor and makes a new contract with the third person who will actually perform. Mere consent to a delegation does not amount to a novation; the obligee must agree to release the original obligor and to hold the new party liable instead.

The circumstances surrounding Forsythia's arrangement with Muddy Fen are probably sufficient to constitute a novation, even though Muddy Fen's release of Violet is not as explicit as it might have been. All three parties signed the "contract" Forsythia sent to Muddy Fen, Muddy Fen agreed that Forsythia would do the work instead of Violet, and Muddy Fen agreed to pay Forsythia directly. Furthermore, Muddy Fen did not reserve itself the right to proceed against Violet if Forsythia failed to perform, and in fact actually would have preferred that Forsythia do the work instead of Violet.

Finally, the boilerplate no-assignment clause in Muddy Fen's contract with Violet is irrelevant, since what occurred was a novation, not an assignment.

Essay VI: Question

(60 Minutes)

Bella Leica is a professional photographer.

(a) Bride-to-be Bree Fondue wanted Bella to photograph her wedding. Bella explained that her basic fee was $500 plus an additional amount depending on which of several wedding photo packages Bree selected. The standard packages ranged in price from $200 to $5,000. Bella's markup on the various packages was 100 percent; that is, Bella paid the photo lab $100 for the package priced at $200, etc. Bree looked at several sample packages and told Bella she liked the $2,000 package. Bella wrote the $2,000 package price into the contract. Before Bree signed, she expressed reservations about committing herself to such an expensive package, so Bella told Bree that in spite of what the contract said, Bree need not commit herself to any particular package now; she could change her mind after the wedding once she had seen the proofs. Bree then signed the contract as written.

As Bella was carrying her photo equipment into the church on Bree's scheduled wedding day, Bree came storming out muttering something about an "insensitive jerk," and was not seen for a week. Bella mailed Bree a bill for $700, itemized as Bella's $500 basic fee plus $200 for the cheapest photo package. She enclosed a note stating, "I know you liked the $2,000 package, but in light of the unfortunate cancellation of your wedding I'm only charging you for the cheapest package."

Bree called Bella and told her she was not going to pay anything, saying, "Don't be ridiculous. You're a *wedding* photographer, right? I hired you to photograph my *wedding*. If there's no *wedding,* I obviously didn't need a *wedding photographer*. The *wedding* was a condition precedent."

Bella sued Bree for $700. Discuss fully the result Bella may expect.

(b) Bella has discovered that many of her customers like a certain style of antique picture frame with wavy glass and that she can charge $30 each for them. She has contracted with her friend F. Lee Marquette—who prowls local tag sales, estate sales, and fairs in search of bargains—to buy for $20 each, any of these frames F. Lee might come upon in his travels. Over the last five years, F. Lee has on the average turned up and sold to Bella a dozen of these frames per month: some months he has not found any; one time he located a box of 100, which Bella gladly bought for $2,000 pursuant to their agreement. Recently F. Lee came upon a forgotten warehouse in the village of Muddy Fen containing a half million of these old frames. He bought the entire lot from the owner for $1 million. The discovery of this warehouse, widely reported in the press, has driven the retail price of the formerly rare frames down to $3. F. Lee tendered all half million frames to Bella, and demanded $10 million. He privately informed his attorney that he knew it might be unrealistic to expect Bella to come up with $10 million, and in fact given the current market he would be happy to continue to sell her a dozen frames per month for $20 each.

If F. Lee pursues the matter in court, what result can he expect? Discuss fully.

(c) Bella's 16-year-old nephew Sol Entean needed a summer job, and he asked Bella if he could work for her for the summer. She told him, "Get a haircut and come to my studio on Monday and I'll try to find something for you to do. I can only pay $6 per hour." On Monday, Sol got out of bed at noon, had a leisurely lunch, got a haircut, and showed up at Bella's studio at 4:30, just as she was preparing to close. Bella lectured him about his irresponsible ways and sent him away, saying, "Nice haircut, though." Sol looked for other work but never did find a summer job.

Sol sued Bella for $3,120, which is the amount he would have earned at $6 per hour, 40 hours per week, for the 13 weeks of summer. Sol claims that Bella understood that he was looking for a job for the entire summer, that his haircut and coming to Bella's studio on Monday constituted consideration for Bella's promise, and that she did not "try to find something for him to do" as she had promised. Bella claims that her statement was too indefinite to constitute a promise, that in any case there was no consideration for it, and that as a 16-year-old, Sol's promise was voidable on grounds of incapacity (the age of majority is 18).

Discuss fully the likely result of Sol's suit.

(d) Bree Fondue's wedding was on again, and she again needed a photographer (see part (a) above). Bree really liked Bella's work and wanted to appease her, so she sent Bella a check for $500 marked "in full satisfaction of amount owed due to canceled wedding." Bree called Bella and told her about the check, and Bella said, "Okay, I'll drop the lawsuit." Bree and Bella then reached a new agreement for Bella to photograph Bree's rescheduled wedding on the same terms as described in (a) above, except that Bella agreed to photograph the rehearsal dinner the evening before the wedding for an additional $100. At the rehearsal dinner, Bree dumped a plate of bratwurst on the head of her beloved and stormed out muttering something about a "low-class clod." Bella and everyone else waited an hour and then left the dinner.

Bella did not bother to show up at the church the next morning. Annoyed with Bree, she wrote on the back of Bree's $500 check, "Under protest. All rights reserved," and deposited the check in the bank.

Bree, it turned out, had reconciled with her intended shortly after everyone left the rehearsal dinner, and the wedding had taken place in the morning as planned. When Bella had not shown up at the church ten minutes before the wedding was to start, Bree hired photographer Iris Di'Afram on an emergency basis instead. Due to the short notice, Iris's rate was double Bella's.

Bree sued Bella for the difference between Bella's rate and Iris's. Bella counterclaimed for $2,100; i.e., the $2,000 difference between Bree's $500 check and the $2,500 Bella could originally have sued Bree for in connection with the first canceled wedding (based on Bree's having signed a written contract that included the $2,000 package), plus $100 for Bella having photographed the rehearsal dinner.

Discuss fully the likely result of the suit.

Worksheet

Essay VI: Model Answer

(a) Bella can probably recover $600 as damages. If the written contract contained a merger clause, she could probably recover $1,500 if she chose to sue for that much.

Bree is mistaken in her contention that her duty to pay Bella was dependent upon the condition precedent of the wedding having taken place. A condition precedent exists where the condition must occur before the obligation to which it is attached becomes an absolute duty. Whether an obligation is conditional is determined by the intent of the parties, whether or not that intent is explicit.

In Bree and Bella's transaction, it appears that neither party considered the possibility that the wedding would not take place. Rather, it appears that both parties intended that Bella would set aside a particular block of time to photograph Bree's wedding, and that she was entitled to be paid for this block of time which she could have devoted to someone else had she been given adequate notice. Furthermore, even if Bree and Bella had entered a contract subject to a condition precedent, Bella would prevail. Where a condition precedent exists, the party whose obligation is subject to the condition may not avoid her obligation by preventing the occurrence of the condition. In Bree's case, the court is unlikely to get into the issue of whether it was Bree or her intended who caused the condition—the wedding—to fail; rather, the court is likely to simply assign the failure of the condition to Bree.

Given that Bree and Bella had entered a valid contract for Bella to photograph Bree's wedding, the next issue concerns the extent of Bella's damages upon Bree's breach. As discussed above, Bella is probably entitled to her basic $500 fee, given her inability to mitigate this portion of her damages by accepting another assignment upon the last-minute cancellation of Bree's wedding. If the written contract is taken as a guide, Bella is also entitled to $2,000 for the wedding photo package Bree selected. If Bella had sued for that much, Bree would successfully argue against Bella being entitled to the full $2,500 reflected in the written contract. First, Bree would argue, Bella is entitled at most to $1,000 in addition to her $500 basic fee, since due to the wedding's cancellation Bella saved having to pay the photo lab anything. That is, according to the written contract, Bree would owe Bella $2,500, but $1,000 of that would have been Bella's payment to the photo lab for its services. Since Bella avoided this expense, her expectation damages are at most $1,500.

Second, Bree would argue that Bella said that Bree could change her mind about which wedding package she selected, even though the written contract indicated that Bree had selected the $2,000 package. Bella would counterargue that the parol evidence rule prevents Bree from now claiming that their agreement was other than is reflected in the written contract. At issue is whether the written contract was integrated; that is, whether the parties intended it to be the final and complete expression of their agreement. If the parties so intended, a party may not introduce a contemporaneous or earlier agreement in an attempt to vary the terms expressed in the integrated writing. Traditionally, a court would look only at the writing itself in determining whether it was integrated. Modern courts are somewhat more liberal, and will consider any relevant evidence in reaching a determination as to whether a written agreement is integrated. A modern court, however, will generally treat as conclusive a "merger clause" stating that the writing containing the clause is the full expression of the parties' agreement.

No mention is made of whether Bella and Bree's contract contains a merger clause. If it does, then Bree is bound by the signed written agreement stating that she would buy the $2,000 package, and Bella would be entitled to the $1,500 damages as discussed above. (But since Bella is only suing for $700, she would be limited to that amount.) If the written contract does not contain a merger clause, the court would probably consider evidence that the real agreement was that Bree could select a package later. That is, if Bella were asked under oath if she told Bree that Bree could change her mind, and if Bella answered truthfully, the court would rule that the parties' true agreement was as Bree alleges.

It appears, however, that the parties intended that Bree would buy some type of package; that is, buying no package was not one of her options. Thus, the court would probably allow Bella her lost profit of $100 on the cheapest package plus her $500 basic fee, for a total of $600.

(b) F. Lee will not be able to insist that Bella buy all 500,000 frames, and he probably cannot insist that she continue indefinitely to buy 12 per month at $20 each.

The contract between Bella and F. Lee will be controlled by Article 2 of the Uniform Commercial Code rather than the common law, since it is a contract for the sale of goods. In particular, the agreement between Bella and F. Lee is an output contract, which is specifically addressed by UCC § 2-306. An output contract is one which measures the quantity of goods to be sold by the seller's output; that is, the buyer agrees to purchase all the goods of a specified type that the seller can produce. UCC § 2-306 specifically states, however, that no quantity unreasonably disproportionate to a stated estimate or prior output may be tendered.

With respect to the contract between Bella and F. Lee, prior output has averaged 12 frames per month over the last 5 years. F. Lee's tendering of 500,000 frames is thus clearly disproportionate, and the court will not enforce a sale of this magnitude. Since F. Lee has indicated a willingness to continue to sell Bella 12 frames per month at $20 per frame, the more difficult question concerns whether he may continue to enforce the contract on these terms.

As described, the contract between Bella and F. Lee does not contain any indication of its duration. Under UCC § 2-309, where a contract for the sale of goods calls for a series of successive performances but is indefinite in duration, the contract is valid for a reasonable time; but unless otherwise agreed it may be terminated at any time by either party. The contract between Bella and F. Lee appears to call for a succession of performances; that is, whenever F. Lee located a worthwhile number of frames, he would tender them to Bella for $20 each. Bella and F. Lee certainly did not intend this arrangement to continue *forever*; rather, they probably intended it to continue as long as it was agreeable to them both. Thus, Bella may terminate the arrangement at any time based on it no longer being agreeable to her. The court would probably, however, require her to purchase F. Lee's current tender of 12 frames at $20 each because she has not yet given him notice of termination.

(c) Bella will probably prevail on the grounds that her conversation with Sol was too indefinite to form a contract. She is incorrect, however, about Sol's minority being a potential grounds for her to disavow the purported contract.

Formation of a contract requires mutual assent. The mechanism for this is the making of an offer followed by an acceptance. The offer must be made with the requisite intent; that is, the offeror must indicate that she is presently willing to enter into an agreement. Additionally, the content of the offer must be sufficiently definite to indicate to the recipient that his assent will suffice to create an agreement. In assessing whether a purported agreement is sufficiently definite, a court will consider whether it is able to fashion a remedy in the event of alleged nonperformance. Where a communication is too indefinite to constitute an offer, it may be better characterized as a solicitation for offers or an offer to enter negotiations.

Bella's statement to Sol is lacking in several respects. It contains no mention of what Sol's duties would be, for how many hours per day, or for how long he would be hired (although an offer omitting this term can be an offer for at-will employment). Bella's statement only promises that she will "try to find something" for Sol to do; by implication, if she cannot find something for him to do, there will be no contract. Her statement that she "can" only pay $6 per hour, literally construed, is not a promise that she "will" pay this amount to Sol. Finally, Bella's requirement that Sol get a haircut and come to her studio suggest that she will consider a visit from him on Monday in the nature of a job interview.

Sol's characterization of the transaction is that Bella's offer was at least for a unilateral contract. That is, Bella offered to try to find something for Sol to do if Sol performed the required acts of showing up on Monday with a haircut. Under this characterization, Bella was seeking a performance, not a promise, in return for her own promise. Once Sol did the required acts, he will argue, Bella became obligated to try to find something for him to do. As discussed above, the best characterization of what Bella had in mind is a job interview, but even if Sol's characterization is accepted he will fail, again because of indefiniteness of the subject matter. The court, in attempting to fashion a remedy for Bella's purported breach, would have a difficult time evaluating whether Bella really "tried," and if she did not, what the parties intended the remedy to be.

While Bella will prevail, her success will have nothing to do with the fact that Sol is a minor. She is mistaken about how minority affects enforceability of a contract.

A contract entered by a minor is voidable by the minor. Such a contract is neither automatically void ab initio, nor is it voidable by the other party who is not a minor. Thus, if Sol and Bella had in fact entered an otherwise enforceable contract, Sol could void it on grounds of minority, but Bella could not.

(d) Bree will probably prevail against Bella. The result depends on whether the court views Bella as having anticipatorily breached her contract with Bree for Bella to photograph Bree's wedding. Bella will probably recover $100 for having photographed the rehearsal dinner, but will not recover anything else beyond the $500 Bree already paid, since Bree's check appears to constitute a valid accord and satisfaction.

An accord and satisfaction occurs when a person to whom a performance is owed agrees to accept a lesser performance than originally called for. A satisfaction occurs when that lesser performance is rendered as agreed. Problems arise when what the obligor party views as an accord and satisfaction is viewed by the obligee party as partial payment of the true amount owed. Even if the obligee agrees to accept the lesser performance, she may attempt to argue later that there was no consideration for her agreement to accept the lesser performance; i.e., the obligor is under a preexisting duty to pay the full amount.

Whether the preexisting duty rule applies—that is, whether the obligee's agreement to accept a lesser amount is supported by consideration—depends on whether the amount of the debt is disputed or undisputed. If undisputed (or liquidated), the preexisting duty rule applies and acceptance of a lesser amount, with no change in the debtor's performance, is not supported by consideration. Where the debt is disputed, the obligee's promise to discharge the entire debt upon payment of a lesser amount is viewed as supported by consideration and will be enforced.

In Bree and Bella's case, the debt appears to be in honest dispute. As discussed in part (a), Bella sued for $700, but Bree asserted that she owed Bella nothing. Thus, Bella's promise to accept a lesser amount than she believes is due is supported by consideration, and is an enforceable accord and satisfaction.

A further reason for holding that a valid accord and satisfaction exists is found in many courts' interpretation of Uniform Commercial Code § 1-207, which permits a party to explicitly reserve rights at the same time she assents to the performance of the other. Difficulties arise where the debtor tenders a check marked "in full satisfaction" of the debt, and the creditor purportedly reserves her rights as allowed by UCC § 1-207 by crossing out the notation and cashing the check. Many courts hold that this use of UCC § 1-207 is invalid, and that a creditor cannot avoid an accord and satisfaction by simply crossing out the "payment in full" notation. Thus Bella, even though she crossed out Bree's "in full satisfaction" language, would still be held to have accepted an accord and satisfaction.

As for Bree's suit against Bella for Bella's failure to show up at the wedding, the result appears to depend on whether Bree's storming out of the rehearsal dinner amounted to anticipatory breach, and what Bella should have done about it. Anticipatory breach may be determined by conduct. A major fight between a couple on the evening before their wedding is probably conduct sufficient to suggest that the wedding will not take place as scheduled.

When faced with anticipatory breach, the aggrieved party has three alternatives:

1. to sue immediately;
2. to urge retraction of the repudiation; or
3. to sue after the time of performance has passed.

Which alternative is most appropriate depends on the circumstances. Here, Bella probably logistically could not have "sued immediately" the night before the wedding. The second alternative appears to have been the most viable, since there was always some possibility, however remote, that Bree and her intended would make up and get married as planned. Bella should have followed up on the fight between the couple either that night or the next morning, and should have demanded assurances one way or the other as to whether the wedding would take place.

Because Bella took no action and just assumed that the wedding would be canceled, she is the one who breached the contract by not showing up the next morning as she promised. Bella is thus liable for Bree's increased expenses in hiring Iris at the last minute.

APPENDIX E

How to Use WESTLAW ®

Contract Law

This card is a quick reference for using WESTLAW to supplement contract law lectures and reading assignments. WESTLAW is West Publishing's computer-assisted legal research service. WESTLAW can complement your book research by quickly and efficiently retrieving information that is not yet available in print or that may be cumbersome to find using books. With WESTLAW you can retrieve relevant documents whether you are starting with a citation, an issue of law or an unusual fact pattern. For more detailed information on WESTLAW, refer to *Discovering WESTLAW: The Essential Guide*, or see your WESTLAW academic representative or student representative about attending a WESTLAW training session.

RETRIEVING DOCUMENTS WHEN YOU HAVE AN ISSUE

There are two search methods you can use on WESTLAW:

Natural Language Search Method (WIN®)

WIN allows you to enter a description of your research issue in standard English. To search for documents using WIN:

1. Access a database by typing **db** followed by the database identifier. For a list of selected databases relating to contract law, see the reverse side of this card.
2. If your current search method is listed as Terms and Connectors, type **nat** and press **Enter**.
3. Enter a description of your issue and press **Enter**. For example, type the following description:
   does supervening destruction of the contract subject matter constitute justified nonperformance

Terms and Connectors Search Method

When you use the Terms and Connectors search method, you enter a query, which consists of key terms from your issue and connectors showing the relationship between these terms. To search for documents using the Terms and Connectors method:

1. Access a database by typing **db** followed by the database identifier. For a list of selected databases relating to contract law, see the reverse side of this card.
2. If your current search method is listed as Natural Language, type **tc** and press **Enter**.
3. Enter your query and press **Enter**. For example, type the following query:
   supervening /s non-performance

RETRIEVING DOCUMENTS WHEN YOU KNOW THE CITATION

Use Find to retrieve a case, statute or law review article when you know its citation. Use Find from almost anywhere in WESTLAW.

▶ Type **fi** followed by the citation. For example, type **fi 884 sw2d 281** or **fi 79 cornell l rev 87**.

SEARCHING WITH TOPIC AND KEY NUMBERS

Each legal issue in a case published by West Publishing is identified, summarized and assigned a topic and key number. West topic and key numbers help you to focus your research and retrieve relevant cases. The Key Number service on WESTLAW contains the entire West Digest System topic and key number outline.

1. Access the Key Number service by typing **key** to see a list of West digest topics.
2. Use Jump to view a specific topic and locate key numbers to assist in your research. To use Jump, press **Tab** until your cursor reaches the Jump marker (> or ▶) preceding the topic you are interested in and press **Enter**. If you use a mouse, position the cursor on the Jump marker and click or double-click.

The following topics may be useful in researching contract law.

8	Accord and Satisfaction	143	Election of Remedies
25	Alteration of Instruments	150	Equity
33	Arbitration	185	Frauds, Statute of
38	Assignments	205h	Implied and Constructive Contracts
42	Assumpsit, Action of	228	Judgment
50	Bailment	246	Lost Instruments
69	Cancellation of Instruments	278	Novation
85	Common Law	316a	Public Contracts
89	Compromise and Settlement	328	Reformation of Instruments
95	Contracts	352	Set-Off and Counterclaim
107	Covenant, Action of		
108	Covenants	358	Specific Performance
113	Customs and Usages	374	Tender
115	Damages		

3. To format a topic and key number search, type the topic number, the letter *k* and the key number. For example, the topic and key number for topic 358, Specific Performance, and key number 88, Good faith of plaintiff in general, is **358k88**.

4. To search using a topic and key number from the Key Number service, type **db** followed by a database identifier and the topic and key number. For example, to run the above topic and key number search in the Federal Commercial Law & Contracts–Cases database (FCML-CS), type **db fcml-cs;358k88**.

SELECTED CONTRACTS DATABASES

	Database Name	Identifier
Federal	Federal Commercial Law & Contracts–Cases	FCML-CS
	Federal Commercial Law & Contracts–U.S. Code Annotated	FCML-USCA
State	Multistate Commercial Law & Contracts–Cases	MCML-CS
	Individual State Commercial Law & Contracts–Cases	XXCML-CS (where XX represents a state's two-letter postal abbreviation)
	State Statutes–Annotated	ST-ANN-ALL
	State Court Rules	RULES-ALL
Combined	Uniform Commercial Code Cases Plus	UCC-CS+
Highlights	WESTLAW Bulletin–U.S. Supreme Court	WLB-SCT
Law Reviews & Texts	Commercial Law & Contracts–Texts & Periodicals	CML-TP
	Commercial Law Journal	COMLJ
	Restatement of the Law–Contracts	REST-CONTR
	Uniform Commercial Code Series (Hawkland)	HAWKLAND
News	Commercial Transactions and Contract News	CMLNEWS
Practice Guides	PLI Commercial Law and Practice Course Handbook Series	PLI-COMM

SEARCHING TEXTS AND PERIODICALS

Recent law review articles are often the best place to begin researching a legal issue because law review articles serve

▶ as an introduction to a new topic or review of a topic with which you are familiar, providing terminology to help in query formulation;

▶ as a tool for retrieving pertinent primary authority, such as cases and statutes; and

▶ in some instances, as persuasive secondary authority.

For example, suppose you want to learn whether silence means acceptance of an offer in contract law.

1. Access the Commercial Law & Contracts–Texts & Periodicals database (CML-TP) by typing **db cml-tp** and pressing **Enter**.

2. Type **nat** and press **Enter**.

3. Type a Natural Language description like the following:
whether silence means acceptance of an offer for a contract

SEARCHING RESTATEMENTS

WESTLAW contains the full text of the American Law Institute's current Restatements of the Law. The *Restatement of the Law Second—Contracts* analyzes current law and explains the most accepted interpretations given by the courts; it also looks at the direction in which the law is moving. Coverage in the Restatement of the Law Second–Contracts database (REST-CONTR) includes the Restatement (Second) of Contracts, appendixes and the current 1995 Cumulative Annual Supplement.

1. To access REST-CONTR, type **db rest-contr** and press **Enter**.

2. To view the table of contents, type the following Terms and Connectors query: **ci(contents)**; or use the Natural Language or Terms and Connectors search method to search for a particular issue. For example, type a Natural Language description like the following:
is a contract voidable if there has been undue influence

VERIFYING YOUR RESEARCH WITH CITATORS

Use Insta-Cite® to see whether your case is good law. Insta-Cite generally displays direct case history within 1-4 hours of when the case is received by West. Direct history traces your case through the appellate process and includes both its prior and subsequent history. Insta-Cite also displays negative indirect history from 1972 to date. Negative indirect history consists of cases outside the direct appellate line that may have a negative impact on the precedential value of your case. To retrieve an Insta-Cite result, type **ic** followed by the case citation: **ic 112 sct 2503**

Use **Shepard's® Citations** to display a comprehensive list of citing references to cases and law review articles. Type **sh** followed by the citation: **sh 112 sct 2503** or **sh 79 cornell l rev 87**

Shepard's on WESTLAW is as current as the most recent publication of Shepard's advance sheets. Therefore, after using Shepard's to retrieve a list of citing cases, you should update the list with more recent citing cases from Shepard's PreView® and Quick*Cite*®.

Use **Shepard's PreView** to update Shepard's Citations. Type **sp** followed by the case citation: **sp 112 sct 2503**

Use **Quick*Cite*** to update Shepard's and Shepard's PreView. Type **qc** followed by the case citation: **qc 112 sct 2503**

Use **WEST*Check*®**, West's automated citation-checking software. WEST*Check* automatically extracts the citations from your brief or other document and retrieves results from Insta-Cite, Shepard's Citations, Shepard's PreView and Quick*Cite*. As a law student, you should receive WEST*Check* software with your WESTMATE® software.

West Documentation. Printed in January 1996.
For additional copies, ask for Item # 1-196-276-9.

Notes

Notes

Notes

Notes

Notes

Notes

Notes

Notes

Notes

Notes

| LAST NAME | FIRST | INITIAL | PERMANENT ADDRESS (if different) |

CURRENT STREET ADDRESS (Do not use P.O. Box — This address used for course materials.)

| CITY | STATE | ZIP | CITY, STATE, ZIP |

( )   ( )
AREA CODE   HOME PHONE   AREA CODE   ALTERNATE PHONE   TELEPHONE

LAW SCHOOL   GRADUATING (MONTH) (YEAR)   E-MAIL ADDRESS

I am enrolling in West Bar Review with a deposit of $ _____

Date: _____

Referred by ❏ Student Rep/Name & School _____

    ❏ Ad ❏ Other

I am interested in bar exam information for the following states:

_____

I plan to take the MPRE in
❏ November 19_____
❏ March   19_____
❏ August   19_____

(to receive MPRE materials a total non-refundable payment of $75 is required)

METHOD OF PAYMENT

❏ CASH ❏ CASHIER'S CHECK ❏ PERSONAL/BUSINESS CHECK AMOUNT _____

TO CHARGE PLEASE COMPLETE: ❏ VISA ❏ MASTERCARD

CARD # _____ EXP. DATE _____

AMOUNT CHARGED TO CREDIT CARD $ _____ CARDHOLDER'S NAME _____

SIGNATURE _____ DATE _____

❏ Bill my law firm
Name _____
Address _____
City _____
State/Zip _____
Attn. _____

FOR OFFICE USE ONLY Total Tuition Due _____ EED _____ Other _____

Date ____	Amount Paid _____	Balance _____	Materials _____	Date Issued _____	Shipped Via _____
Date ____	Amount Paid _____	Balance _____	Materials _____	Date Issued _____	Shipped Via _____
Date ____	Amount Paid _____	Balance _____	Materials _____	Date Issued _____	Shipped Via _____

- -

Thank you for your enrollment in West Bar Review.

STUDENT NAME: _____

COURSE: _____ TOTAL TUITION: _____

AMOUNT PAID: _____ ❏ CASH ❏ CHECK ❏ CC RECEIVED BY: _____

West Bar Review schedules and information will be mailed to you at the above address. If there are changes in your enrollment information, please contact your West Bar Review representative or call 800/693-7822.

LAST NAME _____ **FIRST** _____ **INITIAL** _____

PERMANENT ADDRESS (if different) _____

CURRENT STREET ADDRESS (Do not use P.O. Box — This address used for course materials.) _____

_____

CITY _____ **STATE** _____ **ZIP** _____

CITY, STATE, ZIP _____

( ) _____ ( ) _____

AREA CODE   HOME PHONE   AREA CODE   ALTERNATE PHONE

TELEPHONE _____

LAW SCHOOL _____ **GRADUATING (MONTH) (YEAR)** _____

E-MAIL ADDRESS _____

I am enrolling in West Bar Review with a deposit of $ _____

Date: _____

Referred by ❑ Student Rep/Name & School _____

❑ Ad ❑ Other

I am interested in bar exam information for the following states:

_____

I plan to take the MPRE in
❑ **November**   19_____
❑ **March**   19_____
❑ **August**   19_____

(to receive MPRE materials a total non-refundable payment of $75 is required)

METHOD OF PAYMENT

❑ **CASH** ❑ **CASHIER'S CHECK** ❑ **PERSONAL/BUSINESS CHECK AMOUNT** _____

TO CHARGE PLEASE COMPLETE: ❑ **VISA** ❑ **MASTERCARD**

CARD # _____ **EXP. DATE** _____

AMOUNT CHARGED TO CREDIT CARD $ _____ **CARDHOLDER'S NAME** _____

SIGNATURE _____ **DATE** _____

❑ Bill my law firm

Name _____

Address _____

City _____

State/Zip _____

Attn. _____

FOR OFFICE USE ONLY   Total Tuition Due _____ EED _____ Other _____

Date _____ Amount Paid _____ Balance _____ Materials _____ Date Issued _____ Shipped Via _____

Date _____ Amount Paid _____ Balance _____ Materials _____ Date Issued _____ Shipped Via _____

Date _____ Amount Paid _____ Balance _____ Materials _____ Date Issued _____ Shipped Via _____

- -

Thank you for your enrollment in West Bar Review.

STUDENT NAME: _____

COURSE: _____ TOTAL TUITION: _____

AMOUNT PAID: _____ ❑ CASH ❑ CHECK ❑ CC RECEIVED BY: _____

West Bar Review schedules and information will be mailed to you at the above address. If there are changes in your enrollment information, please contact your West Bar Review representative or call 800/693-7822.